The Taste of Sabbath

the taste of
SABBATH

How to Delight in God's Rest

STUART BRYAN

canonpress
Moscow, Idaho

Published by Canon Press
P.O. Box 8729, Moscow, ID 83843
800.488.2034 | www.canonpress.com

Stuart Bryan, *The Taste of Sabbath: How to Delight in God's Rest*
Copyright © 2009 by Stuart Bryan
Scripture taken from the New King James Version, unless otherwise noted.
All emphases are the author's.

Cover and interior design by Laura Storm.
Printed in the United States of America.

Library of Congress Cataloging-in-Publication Data

Bryan, Stuart (Stuart W.)
  The taste of Sabbath : how to delight in God's rest / Stuart Bryan.
    p. cm.
  ISBN-13: 978-1-59128-068-2 (pbk.)
  ISBN-10: 1-59128-068-0 (pbk.)
  1. Sabbath. 2. Sunday. I. Title.
  BV111.3.B78 2009
  263'.1--dc22

                                        2009038895

09 10 11 12 13 14 15   10 9 8 7 6 5 4 3 2 1

For my parents
who taught me to feast;
And for my wife
with whom I share the feasting.

CONTENTS

Preface

Children rarely turn out the way we expect. In the beginning we receive the bundle and dream over him our images of growth. Then the growth comes and the youth standing by our side is the one imaged by God, not us. "The mind of man plans his way, but God directs his steps." We glance at our child and note, with a start, what God did in the years between.

This book strikes me much the same way. Glancing at it now that it's all grown up, I hardly recognize the swaddling infant I sent off.

She was conceived as a sermon series while I was preaching through the Gospel of Mark. Endeavoring to help my congregation apply Jesus' teaching on the Sabbath in our modern context, I developed a short series on the Sabbath and the Lord's Day. As I studied for the sermons, I was forced to reckon repeatedly with Mark's heavy dependence upon Isaiah 40–66. He self-consciously interprets Jesus' ministry in light of God's promise through Isaiah to vindicate His Name in all the earth. The more I studied Isaiah, the more I came to understand Mark—and the more I understood Mark, the more I understood Jesus—and the more I understood Jesus, the more I understood the Sabbath. Thus the infant was born.

She was sent off to Canon Press, and they were kind enough to nurse and nurture her. The editing work began. Frank Ewert wrote with critiques, suggestions, alterations, and evaluations pushing me to clarify and strengthen the arguments I had made. He recommended changes of organization to clarify thought, kept pestering me about my numerous prepositional phrases, and by and large made a nuisance of himself. He was an excellent editor.

And now the young woman stands before me—where'd she come from? Mark and Isaiah still figure large in her pages, but the discussion is broader and the case, I trust, stronger than originally made. I find myself humbled, giddy, and profoundly grateful—grateful to God who directed the steps.

After reading the book you may yet conclude, "Stronger? I would have hated to see the first draft!" If so, the fault is all mine. But for those who read and appreciate what's written, join with me in giving thanks to the Father who has gifted us so richly and who has qualified us to enter His rest through Christ. Got to love those prepositions!

CHAPTER 1

A Perpetual Ordinance

Introduction

Every Sunday our congregation hosts a question and answer session following the service. We affectionately call it "Filling up the Corners" after an incident in Tolkien's *Fellowship of the Ring*. Bilbo invites his friends and relations to a grand feast in celebration of his "one hundred and eleventieth" birthday.

> After the feast (more or less) came the Speech. Most of the company were, however, now in a tolerant mood, at that delightful stage which they called 'filling up the corners'. They were sipping their favourite drinks, and nibbling at their favourite dainties and their fears were forgotten. They were prepared to listen to anything, and to cheer at every full stop.[1]

[1]J.R.R. Tolkien, *The Fellowship of the Ring* (New York: Houghton Mifflin, 1994), 28.

And so, having feasted on the Word of God in worship, we break out the drinks and dainties (coffee and donuts in our case), sit in a circle, and ask and answer questions about the sermon. After preaching a sermon on the relationship between the Old Testament Sabbath and the Lord's Day, I asked those who could remember what things looked like when there was a broad cultural consensus restricting work on the Lord's Day.

One reported that when he was a child, he distinctly remembered how quiet things were on Sunday. Grocery stores alone were open for business, and most of their aisles were roped off with only necessities offered for sale. But by the time he was a teenager, all that had changed. The restrictions were gone and more and more businesses stayed open. The noise grew.

Why the change? Among the various reasons given, the most poignant was the lack of clear teaching in the Church. The Church always leads culture, and in this area, the Church lost its moorings. Thus, the breakdown of consensus in the Church over the relationship between the Sabbath and the Lord's Day led to the breakdown in our culture at large.

This lack of consensus has not changed in subsequent years. If anything, it has deepened. This to such an extent that, according to N. T. Wright, the Bishop of Durham, most Christians have given up any hope that a renewal of Sunday Sabbath observance will ever emerge in England or America again. Indeed, many would fight against such a proposal.

Diversity of Opinion

Consider, briefly, four of the most common positions articulated by conscientious Christians today. First, some believe the Old Testament Sabbath is completely abolished, and thus no day of the week is different from another. Arguing from Paul's comments in Romans 14, these Christians argue that each individual church is free to establish times for corporate worship at its discretion. It is only a matter of convenience that leads most Christians to choose Sunday as the day for corporate worship.

Others believe, like our first group, that the Old Testament Sabbath is completely abolished, but they insist that in the Christian era it has been replaced by the Lord's Day—a day which has little or no connection with the Old Testament Sabbath. This has been the position of the Roman Catholic church which, with its view of church tradition, is able to argue that such a replacement has divine sanction. Some evangelicals also hold this position and generally argue that the references to worship on the first day of the week in the New Testament substantiate this change.

Still others believe that the Old Testament Sabbath is binding in the exact form in which it was originally given, and that Christians should therefore worship on Saturday. The various "Seventh Day" Christian groups that have emerged in the last couple of centuries advocate this view. Though a minority position in Christendom, many have been persuaded by their arguments and the seventh day churches continue to grow in strength and number.

Finally, some believe—and this will be my contention below—that the Old Testament Sabbath is still binding but has undergone a transformation and been fulfilled in the Lord's Day, the Christian Sabbath. This was the near-unanimous position of the Puritans, both in England and in America. Through their influence and persuasiveness, it became the predominant position in the English speaking world and led to the establishment of Sunday blue laws in some countries. Work on Sunday was taboo; worship expected.

Given this disparity of opinion over the relationship between the Old Testament Sabbath and Christian worship, it is no surprise that Wright expressed such pessimism about the future of Sunday Sabbath observance. Few have hope that it will be renewed. I'm one of those few. The Puritans managed, through the faithful preaching of the Word of God and the beauty of transformed lives, to create a national consensus that favored Sunday Sabbath observance. If God could accomplish this through them, then He can do the same thing through His Church today; particularly if, in our presentation of the case for the Lord's Day, we show its beauty, integrity, and delight.

This book is one small effort to accomplish that task. It does not pretend to be a thorough treatment of the issues surrounding the observance of the Lord's Day. It does not deal with all the relevant biblical texts. It does not deal with all the counter arguments. What it does do is reflect on the beauty of the Sabbath particularly in light of the books of Isaiah and Mark. Why these books? Because I have been preaching on the Gospel of Mark, and Mark depends heavily upon Isaiah for his presentation of the good news about Jesus Christ. Often overlooked because of its relative brevity, the Gospel of Mark is a treasure trove of wisdom and instruction for us as the people of God. Not only does Mark give us a vivid portrayal of the life of our Lord, he repeatedly relates his story back to the expectation for a new exodus proclaimed by Isaiah.[2] In so doing, he shows us how to read and apply the Old Testament in our own day.

Keep Justice

Given the diversity of opinion over the relationship between the Old Testament Sabbath and the Lord's Day, why do I maintain that the Old Testament Sabbath is still binding but has undergone a transformation in the Christian era? It will be helpful to answer this question in two parts. Let us first answer the question

[2]See Rikki E. Watts, *Isaiah's New Exodus in Mark* (Grand Rapids: Baker, 1997).

of the binding nature of the Sabbath and then, in the next chapter, look at why it has been changed to the Lord's Day.

Let's begin with the first question: is weekly Sabbath observance still required of the people of God? Or, stated another way, did God intend for the Sabbath to be a perpetual (continuing) ordinance? To answer this question, it will be helpful to consider Isaiah 56:1–8. Isaiah reveals a number of things about the nature of the Sabbath that will help us to answer our question and understand why the Sabbath command is still binding today.

¹Thus says the Lord:

①"Keep justice, and ⓐdo righteousness,
  For My salvation is about to come,
  And My righteousness to be revealed.
  ²Blessed is the man who does this,
  And the son of man who lays hold on it;
①Who keeps from defiling the Sabbath,
ⓐAnd keeps his hand from doing any evil."

  ³Do not let the son of the foreigner
  Who has joined himself to the Lord
  Speak, saying,
  "The Lord has utterly separated me from His people";
  Nor let the eunuch say,
  "Here I am, a dry tree."
  ⁴For thus says the Lord:
①"To the eunuchs who keep My Sabbaths,
ⓐAnd choose what pleases Me,
  And hold fast My covenant,
  ⁵Even to them I will give in My house
  And within My walls a place and a name
  Better than that of sons and daughters;
  I will give them an everlasting name
  That shall not be cut off.

⁶"Also the sons of the foreigner
Who join themselves to the Lord, to serve Him,
And to love the name of the Lord, to be His servants—
① Everyone who keeps from defiling the Sabbath,
② And holds fast My covenant—
    ⁷Even them I will bring to My holy mountain,
And make them joyful in My house of prayer.
Their burnt offerings and their sacrifices
Will be accepted on My altar;
For My house shall be called a house of prayer for all nations."
⁸The Lord God, who gathers the outcasts of Israel, says,
"Yet I will gather to him
Others besides those who are gathered to him." (Is. 56:1–8)

In this passage God is issuing a two-fold command to the people of Israel in light of His promise to deliver them from exile: "Keep justice, and do righteousness" (v. 1). These two basic commands are repeated in different ways throughout the text. For example, in verse 2 we are told, "Blessed is the man who does this." What is "this"? Keeping justice and doing righteousness. "And the son of man who lays hold on it." What is "it"? Again, keeping justice and doing righteousness. Then notice, in Hebrew parallelism, the way that God restates "keeping justice and doing righteousness" at the end of the verse:

Who keeps from defiling the Sabbath,
And keeps his hand from doing any evil.

According to this parallel, keeping justice means keeping the Sabbath and doing righteousness means keeping one's hand from doing evil. This parallel is repeated throughout verses 1–8. In verse 4 God makes a promise to the eunuchs who (1) "keep My Sabbaths" and (2) "choose what pleases Me, and hold fast My covenant." Again we read in verse 6 that God promises to bless the foreigner who (1) "keeps from defiling the Sabbath" and (2) "holds fast My covenant." Isaiah makes quite clear that "keeping justice" is the equivalent of "keeping the Sabbath."

It may strike us as a bit odd that Isaiah connects the Sabbath with the preservation of justice. But this reveals how out of touch we are with the Sabbath legislation in the Old Testament and how individualistic we are in the way we approach the law—reading it only in light of our own individual lives and not also in light of the broader societal impact that God's laws have. For if we go back to the law, we soon discover that the Sabbath was intimately connected with the preservation of justice in Israel. In particular, the Sabbath was instituted for the benefit of those who could be most easily exploited in society: servants, slaves, and immigrants—in other words, the poor and needy.

We read, for instance, in Exodus 23:12:

> Six days you shall do your work, and on the seventh day you shall rest, *that your ox and your donkey may rest, and the son of your female servant and the stranger may be refreshed.*

Likewise the second giving of the Ten Commandments in Deuteronomy states the reason for the Sabbath command as follows:

> [12]Observe the Sabbath day, to keep it holy, as the LORD your God commanded you. [13]Six days you shall labor and do all your work, [14]but the seventh day is the Sabbath of the LORD your God. In it you shall do no work: *you, nor your son, nor your daughter, nor your male servant, nor your female servant, nor your ox, nor your donkey, nor any of your cattle, nor your stranger who is within your gates, that your male servant and your female servant may rest as well as you.* [15]And remember that you were a slave in the land of Egypt, and the LORD your God brought you out from there by a mighty hand and by an outstretched arm; therefore the LORD your God commanded you to keep the Sabbath day. (Deut. 5:12–15)

In any society, those who are most vulnerable to exploitation are immigrants, who typically do not understand the language and customs well, and slaves or servants, who have very little, if any, freedom. And in the texts above, we see that God is concerned about these very folks. He wanted to protect them from abuse and exploitation and so instituted the Sabbath on their behalf.

This is why, incidentally, when the prophets condemn the people of Israel for violating the Sabbath, they frequently address their exhortations to the leaders of society.

> [6]Look, *the princes of Israel:* each one has used his power to shed blood in you. . . . [8]You have despised My holy things and profaned My Sabbaths. (Ezek. 22:6, 8)

> [25]The conspiracy of *her prophets* in her midst is like a roaring lion tearing the prey; they have devoured people; they have taken treasure and precious things; they have made many widows in her midst. [26]*Her priests* have violated My law and profaned My holy things . . . and they have hidden their eyes from My Sabbaths. (Ezek. 22:25–26)

This is also seen in Isaiah 56. Immediately after Isaiah's words of encouragement to keep the Sabbath and do righteousness, he proceeds to issue a judgment oracle against the leaders in Israel (56:9–12). Why? Because the leaders, princes, nobles, priests, and prophets—or, in our modern context, the politicians, tax collectors, business owners, CEOs, and sometimes even pastors—were those who stood the *most to gain* and the *least to lose* from the violation of the Sabbath. When business happens on the Sabbath, tax revenues increase, tithing from big donors or corporate executives may increase, etc. But note that it is typically not the politicians or the executives themselves that are doing the work—it is the individuals who are subject to their regulation or who are employed by them.

The number of conversations I have personally had with individuals working on Sunday reveals this very thing. "I would love to come to church, pastor, but my manager won't let me off. I have requested several times, but I just don't have enough seniority." The leaders of society stand the most to gain and the least to lose from permitting the violation of the Sabbath.

Notice, then, the first thing that Isaiah tells us about the Sabbath: keeping the Sabbath is the equivalent of upholding justice by providing refreshment and rest for people, particularly the most vulnerable members of society. And here's the question—Is God still concerned about justice? Is he still concerned about the poor and needy? Still concerned about the most vulnerable members of society? These seem like silly questions, don't they? Of course God is still concerned about justice. Of course He is concerned about the poor and needy, about the most vulnerable members of society. James tells us that pure and undefiled religion is this—to care for widows and orphans in their distress (Jas. 1:27). So what would James say to those who refuse to give their employees rest? He would roundly condemn them. He would not be like a blind watchman (cf. Is. 56:10).

Regulate Worship

But perhaps each society is free to uphold justice by providing periods of refreshment and rest in other ways—by using other tools to accomplish the purpose. Why believe that God continues to maintain the need to set apart one specific day a week? Perhaps the weekly Sabbath was wholly and completely a ceremonial command, part of the ceremonial law that passed away (like the distinctions between clean and unclean foods). The problem with this position is that the Old Testament doesn't treat the Sabbath this way; rather, it distinguishes between the Sabbath and other laws which are ceremonial in nature.

We see this in our text from Isaiah 56. In verses 3–7 God announces that when His salvation arrives, it will incorporate folks who have previously been excluded from temple life and full participation in the covenant community and covenant rituals. Who are these folks? Foreigners and eunuchs.

A   ³Do not let the son of the foreigner
    Who has joined himself to the Lord
    Speak, saying,
    "The Lord has utterly separated me from His people";

      B   Nor let the eunuch say,
        "Here I am, a dry tree."

      B'   ⁴For thus says the Lord:
        "To the eunuchs who keep My Sabbaths,
        And choose what pleases Me,
        And hold fast My covenant,
        ⁵Even to them I will give in My house
        And within My walls a place and a name
        Better than that of sons and daughters;
        I will give them an everlasting name
        That shall not be cut off.

A'   ⁶"Also the sons of the foreigner
    Who join themselves to the Lord, to serve Him,
    And to love the name of the Lord, to be His servants—
    Everyone who keeps from defiling the Sabbath,
    And holds fast My covenant—
    ⁷Even them I will bring to My holy mountain,
    And make them joyful in My house of prayer.
    Their burnt offerings and their sacrifices
    Will be accepted on My altar;
    For My house shall be called a house of prayer for
        all nations." (Is. 56:3–7)

The text, with poetic grace and chiastic form, places a lament on the lips of foreigners and eunuchs. But both the foreigners (v. 3a) and the eunuchs (v. 3b) are exhorted not to speak thus. In addition, they are told to take comfort in God's promise to compensate them for their plight—first the eunuchs (vv. 4–5) and then the foreigners (vv. 6–7).

The law had placed certain restrictions on both of these groups. Consider first the restrictions on eunuchs. Not only were they reckoned defective and forbidden to serve as priests (cf. Lev. 21:16ff), but they were even forbidden to "enter the assembly of the Lord," that is, to join with the people of God in the temple worship (cf. Deut. 23:1). In addition, they could not rest in the promise of God to bless their descendants—for they would have none. But here in Isaiah God promises to bless these folks, to grant them a place within his temple and a name even better than offspring.

In other words, the restrictions initially placed on eunuchs are treated as ceremonial laws that would lose their binding character with the coming of God's salvation. But the Sabbath is not placed in this same category. Indeed, their loyalty to the weekly Sabbath was the very thing that would secure these eunuchs a place in the temple. So is the Sabbath simple ceremonial law designed to pass away like the other ceremonial laws? Isaiah implies that the answer is no.

We see the same principle expressed with the foreigners (or Gentiles), who were also restricted from fully entering the temple. In the Old Testament, the temple was surrounded by various courts. The court of the Gentiles was at the outermost limits, followed by the court of the women, then of the men, and then of the priests. Thus, by ceremonial law the Gentiles were kept on the outskirts of covenant life even after they converted. But what does Isaiah announce in this passage? He declares they will be brought into the courts, their sacrifices will be accepted, and they will be fully incorporated into the people of God. The ceremonial restriction upon their participation will pass away. But will the Sabbath? Well, no—like the eunuchs, it is their Sabbath observance that will identify these foreigners as those who will be brought to the "holy mountain" (v. 7).

Let's explore this matter in more detail. Why is the Sabbath not simple ceremonial law? Consider its inclusion in the Ten Commandments. So central was the weekly Sabbath to the life of God's people and to the concern of God for them, that He incorporated it into His covenant document with Israel. Why? Because the fourth commandment answers a pivotal question: when should we gather as a people to worship our God?

Consider also the nature of the first four commandments (cf. Exod. 20:1–8). All of them revolve around worship. The first command ("You shall have no other gods before Me") answers the question, *"Whom are we to worship?"* The answer is God alone: no other deity or creature is worthy of worship. The second command ("You shall not make for yourself a carved image") answers the question, *"What means are we to use in worship?"* The answer is that we are to worship not by means of carved images, but in Spirit and Truth, through the Word of God (cf. Deut. 4). God is too great to be worshiped via idols. The third command ("You shall not take the name of the Lord your God in vain") answers the question, *"In what manner are we to worship?"* The answer is that we are not to worship duplicitously or dishonestly, but reverently and truthfully. God is not ignorant of deceit and treachery. Finally, the fourth command ("You shall remember the Sabbath day, to keep it holy") answers the question, *"When are we to worship?"* It was necessary for the public worship of Israel to be regulated, and God regulates it in this command.

These four commands orient all of Israel around worship because worship always defines culture. What we worship inevitably manifests itself in the priorities we establish, the artwork we produce, the labor we perform, the literature we write, and the technology we develop and utilize. As Van Til insisted, "Culture is religion externalized."[3]

This is precisely why the first four commandments establish a foundation for Israel's worship. They form the living, organic soil out of which the rest of the commands grow. Abandon the proper worship of God and no amount of "moralism" will survive. The commands to honor one's parents, to avoid murder, adultery, theft, false witness, and covetousness soon disappear. They become like branches snipped from the vine—gradually they wither and die even if they're stuck in a vase of water for a time.

Notice then the second thing we learn from Isaiah about the weekly Sabbath: it is not simple ceremonial law. It was included in the Ten Commandments not only to uphold justice, but to regularize the worship of God. So we ask the same question we asked about justice—Is God still concerned about regular worship? Well, duh! He is so concerned about it that He gives us this command in Hebrews: "Do not forsake the assembling of yourselves together as is the habit of some" (Heb. 10:25). Worship is a priority; gathering with the people of God is a priority. And what warning does Hebrews offer to those who fail to gather for the public worship of God? "It is a fearful thing to fall into the hands of the living God" (Heb. 10:31).

Imitate God

So far we have seen that the Sabbath command was given for two reasons: to uphold justice by providing rest and to regularize the public worship of God by making it a weekly event.

[3]Henry Van Til, *The Calvinistic Concept of Culture* (Grand Rapids: Baker Academic [1959, 1972], 2001), 200.

But, some might ask, couldn't worship be regularized in some other way? Why believe that worship has to take place in the Christian era on a specific day each week? Why not biweekly? Monthly? Or why not every eight or nine days? There is, after all, no astronomical significance to a week of seven days. Why is it that Western society—from the days of the Roman hegemony and in company with many others both Christian and non-Christian—has historically observed a seven day week?

We may find some illumination on this matter if we ask another question of Isaiah's text: why were foreigners to keep the Sabbath? The Sabbath, after all, was part of God's covenant with Israel—but other nations weren't part of that covenant. So why does the text require foreigners to keep it? Look at the text again:

> 6"Also the sons of the foreigner
> Who join themselves to the Lord, to serve Him,
> And to love the name of the Lord, to be His servants—
> Everyone who keeps from defiling the Sabbath,
> And holds fast My covenant—
> 7Even them I will bring to My holy mountain,
> And make them joyful in My house of prayer.
> Their burnt offerings and their sacrifices
> Will be accepted on My altar;
> For My house shall be called a house of prayer for all nations."
> (Is. 56:6–7)

A careful study of the Old Testament reveals that foreigners were called to observe the Sabbath because the Sabbath is connected not simply with the Mosaic law but *with creation itself.* The seven day week reflects the activity of God in creation (cf. Gen. 2:2–3). In other words, the Sabbath predates the Mosaic law. This is why we see vestiges of the Sabbath in cultures outside Israel. All cultures had holy days—days set apart for the honor and worship of their deities. Many cultures even had seven day weeks. What the biblical record indicates is that the Sabbath was not created by Mosaic legislation, but rather incorporated into it. The pattern of a weekly day of rest is a creation ordinance connected with the work of God Himself.

> [8]Remember the Sabbath day, to keep it holy. [9]Six days you shall labor and do all your work, [10]but the seventh day is the Sabbath of the LORD your God. In it you shall do no work: you, nor your son, nor your daughter, nor your male servant, nor your female servant, nor your cattle, nor your stranger who is within your gates. [11]*For in six days the LORD made the heavens and the earth, the sea, and all that is in them, and rested the seventh day.* Therefore the LORD blessed the Sabbath day and hallowed it. (Exod. 20:8–11)

> [16]Therefore the children of Israel shall keep the Sabbath, to observe the Sabbath throughout their generations as a perpetual covenant. [17]It is a sign between Me and the children of Israel forever; *for in six days the LORD made the heavens and the earth, and on the seventh day He rested and was refreshed.* (Exod. 31:16–17)

Note that Israel was commanded to observe a seven day week broken into six days of labor and one day of rest because this mirrored God's own action. In other words, one of the principles embodied in the Sabbath was the imitation of God as Creator. God created the world in six days and rested on the seventh—and so, Israel was to do likewise. Israel was to imitate their Creator.

Here is the challenge that Isaiah would level at us: "Is God your Creator? If so, then why don't you imitate Him and observe a weekly day of rest?" As Paul urges us in his letter to the Ephesians, "Therefore be imitators of God as dear children" (5:1).

Conclusion

Isaiah has revealed a number of principles that help us understand the abiding validity of the Old Testament Sabbath. Given that the weekly Sabbath embodied standards of justice that continue in the New Testament era; given that the weekly Sabbath regulated the public worship of God's people, worship that continues to be prioritized in the New Testament; and given that the weekly Sabbath is a creation ordinance that reflects God's own pattern of work and rest which we as Christians are called to imitate, we must conclude that the Sabbath was intended to be a perpetual institution.

As we consider the principles embedded in Isaiah 56, it is worth noting that Jesus uses this very passage to explain and justify His own ministry on at least two occasions. When Jesus cleanses the temple after His triumphal entry into Jerusalem, He condemns the Jews for transforming the place erected as a beacon of hope and salvation for the world into a symbol of oppression and corruption. To make His point, He quotes from Isaiah 56:7: "Is it not written, 'My house shall be called a house of prayer for all nations'? But you have made it a 'den of thieves'" (Mk. 11:17).

Similarly, Jesus alludes to the promise in Isaiah 56:8 ("Yet I will gather to him others besides those who are gathered to him") in order to rebuke the Pharisees' unbelief and to hold out hope for the Gentiles, the "sons of the foreigner" (Is. 56:6). After Jesus heals the man born blind, He instructs the Pharisees about His identity as the Good Shepherd and declares, "And *other sheep I have* which are not of this fold; them also *I must bring,* and they will hear My voice; and there will be one flock and one shepherd" (Jn. 10:16). In both of these passages, Jesus *confirms the abiding validity of the promises held out by Isaiah and exhorts us to learn from the principles embodied in the text.*

Does the Sabbath command continue today? Yes.

CHAPTER 2

From Sabbath to Lord's Day

Introduction

While I was in college in the early 1990s, I took a course entitled "Christianity in America." One of our assignments for the course was to investigate a particular segment of American Christianity after studying its history. We were to contact a specific congregation, interview the pastor and congregants, and determine how connected they were with their historic roots.

I studied Seventh Day Adventism. I interviewed a pastor and his congregation, attended their Sabbath service, and even joined them for a conference that was held at a local Adventist boarding school. The study was fascinating. I discovered that tensions were emerging in the congregation over certain peculiar Adventist practices. For example, Adventism historically rejected all non-functional jewelry. Consequently, Adventists had avoided the exchange of wedding rings, preferring instead to exchange watches. But this historical consciousness was waning: wedding rings were beginning to appear and causing a bit of a ripple in the social fabric.

Despite this and other similar points of tension, one area where they were decidedly unified was the celebration of the seventh day Sabbath. Pastor and congregation alike eagerly supported it. Citing some of the same arguments listed in the previous chapter, all championed the perpetuity of the Sabbath law. They spoke eagerly, pushed books into my hands, and urged me to join them in the practice.

If you have read the last chapter carefully, you may be asking yourself, "If the Sabbath is perpetual, why don't we worship on Saturday? Should we become Seventh Day Adventists? Do they have it right?" Well, quite simply, no.

Moral Law vs. Positive Law

When considering the various laws throughout the Old Testament, we must make a distinction between *moral law* and *positive law*. Moral law (which is sometimes called *natural law*) describes those scriptural commands which proceed from the very nature of God and can never be changed. As the Scottish theologian John Colquhoun remarks,

> The natural law of God, or the law of nature, is that necessary and unchangeable rule of duty which is founded in the infinitely holy and righteous nature of God. . . . The dictates of God's natural law are delivered with authority because they are just and reasonable in their own nature previous to any divine precept concerning them, inasmuch as they are all founded in the infinite holiness, righteousness, and wisdom of His nature.[1]

[1] *A Treatise on the Law and the Gospel* (Morgan: Soli Deo Gloria, 1999), 1–2.

The commands to love one another and to feed the poor as well as the prohibitions against murder, adultery, and perjury would be examples of such laws.

There are other laws, however, which proceed not so much from the nature of God as from the will of God—these are termed *positive law*. Consider, for example, the rite of circumcision. God commanded Abraham to circumcise his children as the sign of the covenant between himself and God. Could God have chosen some other rite to serve as the sign of the covenant? Well, yes, He could have. There is no necessary connection between the sign of circumcision and God's nature. God commanded this particular sign, and so it became obligatory. But note that with the coming of Christ, circumcision is changed, transformed into, and fulfilled by baptism (cf. Col. 2:11–12). God changed the sign of the covenant. Does this mean that God changed? No. Because the nature of the command to circumcise is fundamentally different from the nature of the commands not to murder, not to commit adultery, etc. The former is a positive law while the latter are moral laws.

Given this distinction, we should clearly class the Sabbath as positive law. Worship on a specific day is not intimately intertwined with the nature of God any more than circumcision. God commanded His people to observe Saturday as the seventh day of the week—as the day of rest and the Sabbath—and so it became obligatory. He could have chosen a different day in seven or even created the world in a different number of days.

There is nothing incongruent, therefore, in some changes or modifications being made to the Sabbath commandment. The form of the command can be altered without implying any change in God's character or in the heart of the command. As Colquhoun remarks,

> Those commandments of God which are founded in the holiness and righteousness of His nature are unalterable and perpetually the same; whereas these which are founded on the sovereignty of His will are in themselves alterable, and He may, by His own express appointment, alter them whenever He pleases.[2]

Again, consider circumcision, which has been changed into baptism as a result of the advancement of the Kingdom of God in Christ. It is at least *possible* that the Sabbath could be changed as well.

Good Tidings

When we couple this possibility with the way that the Old Testament speaks about the coming salvation to be wrought by God in Christ, change becomes not just possible but likely. This becomes evident when we compare the reasons given for the institution of the Sabbath with Isaiah's descriptions of the coming salvation in Christ.

Isaiah, more than any other Old Testament book, reflects on the great wonder of God's coming salvation. Chapters 40–66 in particular form the heart of New Testament reflection on the meaning of Jesus' life, death, and resurrection. Even the word "Gospel" or "good tidings," which we associate with the accounts of Jesus' life, receives its origin in this section of Isaiah.

> O Zion,
> You who bring good tidings,
> Get up into the high mountain;
> O Jerusalem,
> You who bring good tidings,

[2]Ibid., 2–3.

Lift up your voice with strength,
Lift it up, be not afraid;
Say to the cities of Judah, "Behold your God!" (Is. 40:9)

What was this "Gospel" or "good tidings" that Isaiah announced? That one day God was going to manifest His power and sovereignty by saving His people. Isaiah 39 had closed with the solemn announcement that, because of Hezekiah's sin, the city of Jerusalem would be destroyed and its inhabitants taken into exile in Babylon. The "good tidings" of chapters 40–66 was that God would act to rescue His people from this exile.

But something startling happens in Isaiah's account. The exile of Israel becomes a matter of poetic reflection on the exile of all mankind. Since the Fall all men—Jew and Gentile alike—were in exile, separated from God because of their sin and rebellion. And so Isaiah announces not only that Israel would be restored from exile through Cyrus the Great of Persia (e.g., Is. 45:1–7), but that all humanity would be restored through His chosen Servant (cf. Is. 42:1–9; 49:1–12; 50:4–9; 52:13–53:12). God would bring all men out of their darkness and blindness, their imprisonment and deafness. He would "restore the earth" (49:8). Why? So that His Name would no longer be defamed among the nations; so that the glory which Jew and Gentile alike were giving to idols would be given to Him (cf. 42:5–9).

After reflecting on these promises in Isaiah, many Israelites concluded that Cyrus and the Servant were going to arrive at the same time. Consequently, when Israel returned to the land following Cyrus' decree, there were huge expectations (cf. Ezra).

The problem was that Israel had failed to repent during their exile; they had continued to transgress against the Lord and to rebel against His commands. And so God announced to the prophet Daniel, who was in exile with the rest of the Jews, that Israel's seventy years of captivity would be multiplied by seven (cf. Dan. 9:1–27)—the very thing He had threatened through Moses (cf. Lev. 26:18, 21, 24, 28).

When the Israelites returned from exile at the command of Cyrus, they experienced the fulfillment of this delay. No Servant arose. Sin and rebellion were still huge problems. The leaders of Israel realized that Israel was still in captivity. Even though they were physically in the land, they were still in exile. They knew that they were in need of another Exodus—and this one, they concluded rightly, would be accomplished by the Servant, the full-orbed Anointed of the Lord, the Messiah.

The "good tidings" of the salvation accomplished by Cyrus became a picture of the greater deliverance that would be accomplished by the Servant of the Lord. The Servant would really lead Israel out of exile; He would truly restore her. And indeed, Isaiah announces repeatedly, He would restore not just Israel but the whole earth. In other words, chapters 40–66 declare two deliverances that reinforce one another—one through Cyrus and another through the Servant.

Therefore He Blessed the Sabbath Day

How does Isaiah 40–66 help us understand why the Sabbath has been changed to the Lord's Day? If we compare the way that Isaiah speaks of this coming salvation in Christ with the justifications given for the Sabbath command, we come to realize that some change is not just possible but likely.

First, consider the two distinct justifications for the institution of the Sabbath that are associated with the two different accounts of the Ten Commandments. The first account occurs in Exodus and connects the Sabbath directly with creation. The Israelites are instructed to rest one day in seven because God created the world in six days, and on the seventh He rested.

[8]Remember the Sabbath day, to keep it holy. [9]Six days you shall labor and do all your work, [10]but the seventh day is the Sabbath of the LORD your God. In it you shall do no work: you, nor your son, nor your daughter, nor your male servant, nor your female servant, nor your cattle, nor your stranger who is within your gates. [11]*For in six days the LORD made the heavens and the earth, the sea, and all that is in them, and rested the seventh day.* Therefore the LORD blessed the Sabbath day and hallowed it. (Exod. 20:8–11)

In the Deuteronomy account, however, the link with creation is not stated. Instead, the Israelites are commanded to rest one day in seven because God had rescued them from the land of Egypt, and so they were to extend this same pity toward their servants, slaves, and livestock. Thus, Deuteronomy connects the Sabbath directly with the Exodus from Egypt—with redemption.

[12]Observe the Sabbath day, to keep it holy, as the LORD your God commanded you. [13]Six days you shall labor and do all your work, [14]but the seventh day is the Sabbath of the LORD your God. In it you shall do no work: you, nor your son, nor your daughter, nor your male servant, nor your female servant, nor your ox, nor your donkey, nor any of your cattle, nor your stranger who is within your gates, that your male servant and your female servant may rest as well as you. [15]*And remember that you were a slave in the land of Egypt, and the LORD your God brought you out from there by a mighty hand and by an outstretched arm;* therefore the LORD your God commanded you to keep the Sabbath day. (Deut. 5:12–15)

What these two passages reveal is that the Sabbath command was linked both to Creation and to Redemption. How does comparing these two justifications for the Sabbath with Isaiah's "good tidings" help us understand why the Sabbath has been changed into the Lord's Day?

A New Creation

First, Isaiah frequently invokes creation language to describe the work that God was going to achieve through His Servant. The beginning of this imagery is found in Isaiah 51. In verses 12 and 13, God rebukes the Israelites for fearing men and imagining perhaps that the nation of Babylon would be too great for God, the Maker of all things, to conquer. He promises that in bringing the captive exiles home, He will protect them and lay the foundations of a new heavens and earth.

> And I have put My words in your mouth;
> I have covered you with the shadow of My hand,
> That I may plant the heavens,
> Lay the foundations of the earth,
> And say to Zion, "You are My people." (Is. 51:16)

This allusion to a new creation becomes explicit later in Isaiah.

> [17]For behold, I create new heavens and a new earth;
> And the former shall not be remembered or come to mind.
> [18]But be glad and rejoice forever in what I create;
> For behold, I create Jerusalem as a rejoicing,
> And her people a joy.
> [19]I will rejoice in Jerusalem,
> And joy in My people;
> The voice of weeping shall no longer be heard in her,
> Nor the voice of crying. (Is. 65:17–19; cf. 66:22–23)

In other words, Isaiah declares, the return from exile accomplished by the Servant of the Lord will be so remarkable that it will be a re-creation of the world.

As indicated earlier, the Gospel of Mark goes to great pains to demonstrate that Jesus came to fulfill the promises that God made in Isaiah 40–66. Mark opens his gospel by quoting Isaiah 40:3:

The voice of one crying in the wilderness:
"Prepare the way of the LORD;
Make straight in the desert
A highway for our God."

From there, Mark goes on to demonstrate that the promises God had issued throughout those chapters are fulfilled in
Jesus. The time of waiting is over. The long awaited Kingdom
of God, God's reign on earth through the Messiah, has come
(cf. Dan. 2:34–35, 44–45; Mk. 1:14–15). The Son of Man now
has authority on earth to forgive sins (cf. Mk. 2:10) because He
has given His life a ransom for many (cf. Mk. 10:45).

The message of Jesus was not that the kingdom had been
postponed. That disquieting announcement had been delivered
years before through Daniel. Jesus came to declare that in Him
the Kingdom had come. He was the long-awaited one, come
to plunder the property that the evil one had stolen from the
Creator (cf. Is. 49:24–25 with Mk. 3:27). He was the bridegroom, come to rejoice over His bride (cf. Is. 62:1–5 with Mk.
2:19ff). He came to His own, as the Apostle John declares, but
His own did not receive him (Jn. 1:11). Why? Because the
Kingdom that He announced was not coming in the way many
Jews had imagined.

Many had taught that when the Kingdom would come, it
would arrive in one fell swoop: the enemies of God would be
routed and Jerusalem exalted in one dramatic moment. Jesus
overturns this teaching. The Kingdom is not like a hydrogen
bomb that annihilates everyone in its wake except those in the
lead refrigerator. Rather, it is like a seed that is first planted,
then grows, and is finally reaped (cf. Mk. 4:26–29).

What this all means is that in Christ, the New Creation
anticipated by Isaiah has arrived. The Kingdom of God has in-
truded into human history and the world has been fundamentally

remade. All things have been made new; therefore, if any man is in Christ, he is a new creation (cf. 2 Cor. 5:17). The message of the New Testament is that the powers of the age to come have entered into human history in such a startling way that there is a New Creation.[3]

Given that the New Creation of Isaiah has arrived in Christ, is it not reasonable to pose the question, "Since Exodus associates the seventh day Sabbath with the old creation, is the Sabbath transformed by the dawn of this *new creation?*"

A New Redemption

A similar question arises when we move from the first giving of the Ten Commandments to the second. As we saw, Deuteronomy links the seventh day Sabbath with the Exodus from Egypt and Isaiah characterizes the coming salvation as a new and greater redemption, a New Exodus.

> [14]Thus says the Lord, your Redeemer,
> The Holy One of Israel:
> "For your sake I will send to Babylon,
> And bring them all down as fugitives—
> The Chaldeans, who rejoice in their ships.
> [15]I am the Lord, your Holy One,
> The Creator of Israel, your King."
>
> [16]Thus says the Lord, who makes a way in the sea
> And a path through the mighty waters,
> [17]Who brings forth the chariot and horse,
> The army and the power

[3]The extent to which Jesus believed the prophecies of the new creation to be fulfilled in his ministry is revealed in his use of Isaiah 66:14–16, 24 to warn the disciples of the fate of those who caused others to stumble (cf. Mk. 9:42–50). In the New Creation, during the rule of the Son of Man, idolatry will be systematically destroyed and punished (cf. Ps. 2; 1 Cor. 11:27–34).

(They shall lie down together, they shall not rise;
They are extinguished, they are quenched like a wick):
[18]"Do not remember the former things,
Nor consider the things of old.
[19]Behold, I will do a new thing,
Now it shall spring forth;
Shall you not know it?
I will even make a road in the wilderness
And rivers in the desert.
[20]The beast of the field will honor Me,
The jackals and the ostriches,
Because I give waters in the wilderness
And rivers in the desert,
To give drink to My people, My chosen.
[21]This people I have formed for Myself;
They shall declare My praise. (Is. 43:14–21)

Notice the way in which Isaiah describes the return from exile in Babylon (v. 14) in language reminiscent of the Exodus (v. 16–17). Recall also that this return from exile is symbolic of the greater redemption to be accomplished by the Servant of the Lord. Consequently, the Servant's work is described in Exodus language.

[7]Thus says the LORD,
The Redeemer of Israel, their Holy One,
To Him whom man despises,
To Him whom the nation abhors,
To the Servant of rulers:

"Kings shall see and arise,
Princes also shall worship,
Because of the LORD who is faithful,
The Holy One of Israel;
And He has chosen You."

[8]Thus says the LORD:

"In an acceptable time I have heard You,
And in the day of salvation I have helped You;
I will preserve You and give You
As a covenant to the people,
To restore the earth,
To cause them to inherit the desolate heritages;
[9]That You may say to the prisoners, 'Go forth,'
To those who are in darkness, 'Show yourselves.'

"They shall feed along the roads,
And their pastures shall be on all desolate heights.
[10]They shall neither hunger nor thirst,
Neither heat nor sun shall strike them;
For He who has mercy on them will lead them,
Even by the springs of water He will guide them.
[11]I will make each of My mountains a road,
And My highways shall be elevated.
[12]Surely these shall come from afar;
Look! Those from the north and the west,
And these from the land of Sinim." (Is. 49:7–12)

The language in verses 9 and 10 is clearly reminiscent of God's provision for Israel as they wandered through the wilderness after their departure from Egypt. In other words, the Servant's work is also a New Exodus.[4]

Isaiah is not the only prophet to describe the return from exile with imagery from the Exodus. Like Isaiah, Jeremiah promised that one day God would rescue His people from exile.

[4]Later, Isaiah recalls God's great power in the Exodus as the basis upon which he calls God to act again in fulfillment of His promises (Is. 63:7–64:5). Interestingly, in describing Jesus' baptism, Mark uses language reminiscent of Isaiah's plea that God "would rend the heavens" and "come down" (Is. 64:1). Mark tells us that when Jesus was baptized, the heavens "were torn open" and the Spirit of God "came down" in the form of a dove upon Jesus (cf. Mk. 1:10).

[14]"Therefore behold, the days are coming," says the LORD, "that it shall no more be said, 'The LORD lives who brought up the children of Israel from the land of Egypt,' [15]but, 'The LORD lives who brought up the children of Israel from the land of the north and from all the lands where He had driven them.' For I will bring them back into their land which I gave to their fathers." (Jer. 16:14–15)

Jeremiah describes the return from exile as a new and greater redemption that would be so momentous that the original Exodus would no longer be remembered. In Jesus, Mark declares that this redemption has come to fruition. The New Exodus has dawned.

Have you ever wondered why we no longer celebrate the three annual feasts and festivals of the Old Testament—Passover, Weeks, and Tabernacles? Jeremiah hints at the answer. Those feasts and celebrations were given to commemorate the deliverance which God accomplished for our fathers in the Exodus—rescuing them from Egypt (Passover), giving them the law (Weeks), and preserving them through the wilderness (Tabernacles). But that deliverance, as glorious as it was, pales when compared to the deliverance which has been accomplished for us through the ministry of our Lord Jesus Christ. This is why the Church has historically developed major Christian feasts that center around the life of our Great Redeemer, the Lord Jesus Christ—Christmas, Epiphany, Easter, Ascension, Pentecost. In these celebrations we declare, "The Lord lives who brought us up out of the darkness of sin and slavery and into the light of righteousness and freedom through our Lord Jesus Christ" (cf. v. 15).

Now apply this same reasoning to the weekly Sabbath. The original Sabbath was given, according to Deuteronomy, to commemorate the Exodus from Egypt. Yet Jeremiah anticipated a day in which God's people would no longer celebrate that

Exodus because it would *pale in comparison* to the new Exodus that God would accomplish. Given this, is it not reasonable to ask the question, "What happens to the Sabbath—an institution so intimately connected with the first redemption—with the arrival of the *new redemption?*"

The First Day of the Week

When we come to the New Testament record with these questions rummaging about in our brains, our lurking suspicions are confirmed. A change does take place. The people of God begin to celebrate the New Creation and the New Exodus on the day in which that reality was introduced. The Sabbath is changed from Saturday to Sunday, the day on which Christ rose from the dead and rested from His labors over the evil one.

Note this in the Scriptures. The Gospels are careful to record that Jesus rose on the first day of the week (Mt. 28:1; Mk. 16:1–2; Lk. 24:1, 13; Jn. 20:1, 19). Then, John tells us, the next time Jesus appears to the disciples en masse is eight days later— again on a Sunday (Jn. 20:26).[5] Subsequently, Jesus pours out His Spirit on the day of Pentecost, a Sunday. And Peter explains the significance of this event by appealing to the resurrection of Jesus as the day that the Messiah was raised up to sit on his throne (Acts 2:30–31). The resurrection, in other words, has transformed the world: the Messiah is now Lord and Christ and the outpouring of the Spirit is proof. Each of these incidents emphasizes again and again that Sunday is the day of the New Creation, the New Redemption, the remaking of the world.

---

[5] The Jews and the Romans counted inclusively. Consequently eight days later would be counted Sunday (the day of the resurrection), Monday, Tuesday, Wednesday, Thursday, Friday, Saturday, Sunday (day 8).

So, what did the disciples do? They began to meet on the first day of the week, doing the very things that the original Sabbath was intended to embody.

First, they upheld justice. The early church considered helping the poor to be of great importance (cf. Gal. 2:10). One of the major events in the Roman world at the time, anticipated by the Christian prophet Agabus, was a major famine on the land of Israel. Paul endeavored to coordinate assistance for those in Jerusalem from the Christians elsewhere, both as an extension of mercy and as a witness to the legitimacy of his ministry among the Gentiles. And so he wrote to the Corinthians, instructing them in this matter:

> [1]Now concerning the collection for the saints, as *I have given orders* to the churches of Galatia, so you must do also: [2]On the first day of the week let each one of you lay something aside, storing up as he may prosper, that there be no collections when I come. (1 Cor. 16:1–2)

Notice that this was something Paul was mandating to the churches and that his command to the Corinthians was not an isolated command: he had already given the same instruction to the Galatians. These churches were to set aside funds *on the first day of the week* for the benefit of the Jerusalem saints. Why? Because this was the day of the New Creation, the New Redemption. This was the new one day in seven. This was the new Sabbath, the Christian Sabbath. What better day to keep justice by assisting the most vulnerable members of society through offerings?

Second, they met on the first day of the week to establish a regular time for corporate worship. Acts 20:7 declares: "Now on the first day of the week, when the disciples came together to break bread, Paul, ready to depart the next day, spoke to them and continued his message until midnight." So in this passage we find the disciples gathering together to break bread[6] and listen to the teaching of Paul. In other words, we have a gathering for corporate worship. This gathering is patterned around the weekly worship in the Jewish synagogues, for Luke's wording, "gathering together," is literally, in the Greek, "synagogue-ing."

The Lord's Day

This transformation from the seventh day to the first is confirmed when we come to the book of Revelation where John says in 1:10, "I was in the Spirit on the Lord's Day, and I heard behind me a loud voice, as of a trumpet." The Lord's Day was Sunday, the day on which the Lord rose from the dead and rested from His fight over the enemy. Why call it the "Lord's" Day? Because it is His day, the day set apart for the worship and honor of our great God and Savior who has recreated the world and redeemed His people; the day set apart to provide for the poor and needy by giving offerings and providing rest and refreshment; the day set apart one in seven to reflect our recreation in the image of Christ. The Lord's Day is the Christian Sabbath.

Interestingly enough, Psalm 118 also talks about the Lord's Day as the fulfillment of all that the Jewish Sabbath prefigured. This Psalm is one of the most frequently quoted psalms in the New Testament and alludes clearly to the crucifixion and resurrection of our Lord. Listen to verses 22–23:

> [22]The stone which the builders rejected
> Has become the chief cornerstone.
> [23]This was the LORD's doing;
> It is marvelous in our eyes.

---

[6]In the book of Acts, "breaking bread" refers to participation in the Lord's Supper (cf. Acts 2:42).

These verses are frequently used both by Jesus and the Apostles to explain Jesus' identity and ministry. So when was the stone (our Lord Jesus) rejected by the builders (the leaders in Israel like the chief priests and Pharisees)? The stone was rejected when Jesus was handed over to the Romans and crucified. And when did Jesus become the chief cornerstone? When He rose from the dead and was declared, by His resurrection, to be the Son of God with power (cf. Rom. 1:4). This deed of the Lord, the psalmist declares, is marvelous in our eyes, for the vindication of our Messiah through the resurrection is astounding and world-transforming.

So as the people of God, what should our response be to the resurrection of the cornerstone? Verse 24 of Psalm 118 declares: "This is the day the LORD has made; we will rejoice and be glad in it." This is the day the stone became the cornerstone: Sunday, resurrection day, vindication day, the Lord's Day. The Lord's Day is a day of feasting and rejoicing, for in it our Christ was vindicated. Therefore, in it we find the fulfillment of the Jewish Sabbath.[7]

---

[7]Church history offers a great confirmation of this truth. Since the time of Christ, the Church has displayed near-unanimous consent that Christian worship is to happen on the Lord's Day. While this is neither a standalone argument, nor a firm basis on which to argue that the Lord's Day ought to be the Christian Sabbath, it can nevertheless serve to buttress our contention that with the resurrection of Christ the public day of worship and rest has been altered. For example, the second century theologian Justin Martyr remarks in his *First Apology,* "On the day called Sunday there is a meeting of all believers who live in the town or the country, and the memoirs of the apostles, or the writings of the prophets, are read for as long as time will permit... We hold our common assembly on Sunday because it is the first day, on which God put to flight darkness and chaos and made the world; and on the same day, Jesus Christ our Saviour rose from the dead." As quoted in N. R. Needham, *2000 Years of Christ's Power, Part One: The Age of the Early Church Fathers* (London: Grace Publications Trust, 2002), 66–67.

What is the Jewish Sabbath?

But what, then, do we do with Paul's remarks in Romans 14 that tell us that no one day is inherently superior to another? How are we to understand Colossians 2:16, where Paul tells us that we are to let no one stand as our judge in reference to a new moon, or a festival, or Sabbaths? Do these passages undermine our case that the Lord's Day should be considered the Christian Sabbath? No.

Remember that the Old Testament contained various feast days and celebrations in addition to the weekly Sabbath. Frequently, it is these celebrations that are in view, and their termination is not disputed. As Jeremiah predicted (Jer. 16), the celebrations of the original Exodus would terminate once the New Exodus occurred. Romans 14, in particular, seems concerned with these feasts. Paul's conclusion is that these feasts are no longer obligatory, but neither are they banned. Jewish Christians who had celebrated them throughout the course of their lives were free to continue that practice, provided that they did not require their Gentile brothers to participate.

But let us say that Paul is explicitly addressing the weekly Sabbath. Do his comments undermine our case? I don't believe so for two reasons. First, Paul's argument is not against the Sabbath per se, but against the way it was being abused. The Colossians, in particular, were being taught that the keeping of various religious rituals—among them the Sabbath—was necessary to attain salvation. Paul condemns such teaching, declaring that such moralism and ritualism cannot solve man's fundamental problem—estrangement from God. Since only Christ can reconcile us with the Father, festivals, foods, and angelic speculations are of no value. However, Paul's rebuke does not undermine a biblical approach to the Lord's Day, for celebrating the Lord's Day is not how we gain God's approval. Rather, it is precisely because God has approved and delivered us that we can and do celebrate the weekly Sabbath.

But second, and even more relevant, it is important to remember that we do not observe the Jewish Sabbath but the Lord's Day, the Christian Sabbath. Consequently, Paul's polemic against the Sabbath is similar to his polemic against circumcision. What is circumcision? Nothing. What is the Jewish Sabbath, the Saturday Sabbath? Nothing. Circumcision is no longer obligatory for the people of God and neither is the Saturday Sabbath. Both have given way to greater realities now that the Kingdom of God in Christ has arrived. Circumcision finds its correlative in baptism and the Saturday Sabbath in the Lord's Day.[8]

It seems just to conclude that not only is the Old Testament Sabbath commandment a perpetual ordinance, but it has also been transformed into and fulfilled by the Lord's Day. Through Christ the new heavens and the new earth, as well as the new redemption, have come. There is a New Creation and a New Exodus, and it is this that we celebrate every Lord's Day.

---

[8] John Frame's observation is trenchant: "I think the best suggestion is that Paul is here addressing a controversy over the Jewish seventh-day Sabbath. The Jewish Christians generally observed the seventh-day Sabbath and then worshiped Jesus on the first day. Some of the Gentile Christians evidently attended the first-day celebration of the resurrection, but did not observe the seventh-day rest. In actual fact, the seventh-day Sabbath was no longer binding. God, Jesus, and the apostles had warranted first-day worship, and, implicitly, a first-day Sabbath" (*The Doctrine of the Christian Life* (Phillipsburg: P&R, 2008), 569. Frame's complete treatment of the fourth commandment is worth reading.

CHAPTER 3

Lord of the Sabbath

Introduction

Rollo, ancestor of the famed William the Conqueror, was in high spirits. With a large band of lusty and reckless followers, he had managed to bring the King of France, Charles the Simple, to terms. In exchange for peace, Rollo was granted the territory of Normandy—provided that he do homage to Charles, marry Charles' daughter, and convert to the Christian faith.

When it came time for the first step, however, difficulties arose. The traditional ceremony of homage involved a number of symbolic rites: the subject would kneel before the king, place his hands together between the king's hands, and swear allegiance. After the oath was sworn, the subject finished the ceremony by kissing the foot of the king, who would wear a special slipper for the occasion. But Rollo absolutely refused to perform this last act.

Kissing the slippered foot of one's superior was not uncommon in the medieval world. Sovereigns were often called upon to kiss the foot of the Popes as a sign of loyalty to the Holy See. But no amount of persuasion could induce Rollo to submit to the practice. Finally, a compromise was achieved: one of Rollo's courtiers would kiss the king's foot in his stead.

As the courtier advanced, however, he greatly bungled the job. When he lifted the king's foot and kissed the slipper, the courtier lifted too high and upset the king's chair, sending the monarch sprawling to the floor. At this Rollo's companions laughed. Charles was powerless to avenge the insult, however; Rollo was simply too powerful. Once the ceremony was complete, Rollo was baptized, married Charles' daughter, and assumed the title Duke of Normandy.

Rollo's humiliation of Charles the Simple helps highlight the connection between principles and ceremonies. Every rite entails a certain set of principles which it is supposed to embody. However, it is always possible to separate the action from its principle and thus do violence to one or the other (as Rollo did while paying homage to Charles). The New Testament reveals that this is precisely what the scribes and Pharisees did with the Sabbath.

Principles and Ceremonies

Before we can fully appreciate the way in which the scribes and Pharisees distorted the Sabbath, it will be helpful to unfold Old Testament reflection on this distinction between principles and ceremonies. Influenced by the pagan religions surrounding them, many Israelites believed that they could simply manipulate God into hearing them by correctly performing religious rituals. They reasoned that personal righteousness was far less important than sacred ceremonies. Consequently, even in times of great national apostasy, these Israelites were extremely conscientious in their performance of religious rites (cf. Zeph. 1:4–5).

This ritualistic mentality was wholly antithetical to the expectations God laid out in the Old Testament. Ceremonies were always far less important than the principles which they embodied. The psalms frequently meditated on this:

> [6]Sacrifice and offering You did not desire;
> My ears You have opened.
> Burnt offering and sin offering You did not require.
> [7]Then I said, "Behold, I come;
> In the scroll of the book it is written of me.
> [8]I delight to do Your will, O my God,
> And Your law is within my heart." (Ps. 40:6–8)

> [7]Hear, O My people, and I will speak,
> O Israel, and I will testify against you;
> I am God, your God!
> [8]I will not rebuke you for your sacrifices
> Or your burnt offerings,
> Which are continually before Me.
> [9]I will not take a bull from your house,
> Nor goats out of your folds.
> [10]For every beast of the forest is Mine,
> And the cattle on a thousand hills.
> [11]I know all the birds of the mountains,
> And the wild beasts of the field are Mine.

> [12]If I were hungry, I would not tell you;
> For the world is Mine, and all its fullness.
> [13]Will I eat the flesh of bulls,
> Or drink the blood of goats?
> [14]Offer to God thanksgiving,
> And pay your vows to the Most High. (Ps. 50:7–14)

Moreover, the prophets frequently denounced Israel for their "faithful" performance of rituals. Amos, for instance, records the declaration of the Lord to Israel:

> [21]I hate, I despise your feast days,
> And I do not savor your sacred assemblies.
> [22]Though you offer Me burnt offerings and your grain offerings,
> I will not accept them,
> Nor will I regard your fattened peace offerings.
> [23]Take away from Me the noise of your songs,
> For I will not hear the melody of your stringed instruments.
> [24]But let justice run down like water,
> And righteousness like a mighty stream. (Amos 5:21–24)

Of course, the answer was not to abandon these rites and rituals altogether. Rather, God required the Israelites to practice them from the heart, to perform them in righteousness and faith. When they failed, God rejected their offerings and declared that He hated their festivities. Unless the principles that upheld and supported the ceremonies were honored, the rituals were useless; indeed, more than useless, they were destructive.

> [12]When you come to appear before Me,
> Who has required this from your hand,
> To trample My courts?
> [13]Bring no more futile sacrifices;
> Incense is an abomination to Me.
> The New Moons, the Sabbaths, and the calling of assemblies—
> I cannot endure iniquity and the sacred meeting.
> [14]Your New Moons and your appointed feasts
> My soul hates;
> They are a trouble to Me,
> I am weary of bearing them.
> [15]When you spread out your hands,
> I will hide My eyes from you;
> Even though you make many prayers,

I will not hear.
Your hands are full of blood.
[16]Wash yourselves, make yourselves clean;
Put away the evil of your doings from before My eyes.
Cease to do evil,
[17]Learn to do good;
Seek justice,
Rebuke the oppressor;
Defend the fatherless,
Plead for the widow. (Is. 1:12–17)

While the Scriptures routinely denounce the faithless performance of rituals, they do not condemn the opposite. There were times when the principles were upheld and the specific ritual was not. This did not necessarily make the ceremony unimportant or irrelevant, but it did indicate that the weightier matter was the principle underlying the ritual. So David confesses his sin with Bathsheba and declares:

[16]For You do not desire sacrifice, or else I would give it;
You do not delight in burnt offering.
[17]The sacrifices of God are a broken spirit,
A broken and a contrite heart—
These, O God, You will not despise. (Ps. 51:16–17)

The truth in this meditation is witnessed in God's mercy to the people of Nineveh. Although they "believed God" (Jon. 3:5) and repented in sackcloth and ashes, they presumably did not accompany this repentance with the sacrifices prescribed in the Mosaic law since they were ignorant of them. God did not despise their broken and contrite spirits.

We see a similar principle outlined in Malachi. Though God's law clearly required that the sacrifices brought to Him be the best of the flock, perfect and without blemish (cf. Lev. 22:22), the Israelites were bringing him lame and sick animals

(1:7–9). God rebukes this practice and bemoans the lack of a priest in Israel who would shut the doors of the Temple to prevent such sacrifices from being offered (1:10). But were a priest to do so, technically he would be breaking the law. The law, after all, commanded that sacrifices be offered. The implication of Malachi's text, however, is that such a priest would be obeying the law on a much more fundamental level. For what was more important, sacrificing an animal that pictured God's hatred of sin and His promise to remove it through Christ or hatred of sin and trust in the God who would remove it? Ideally this was a false dilemma; the two were to go together. But when push came to shove, a righteous priest would choose the latter and forbid the sacrifices altogether.

The consistent message of Scripture, therefore, is that the principles which lie behind any ritual are of far greater importance than the ritual itself. As Jesus insists, there are weightier matters of the law.

> Woe to you, scribes and Pharisees, hypocrites! For you pay tithe of mint and anise and cummin, and have neglected the weightier matters of the law: justice and mercy and faith. These you ought to have done, without leaving the others undone. (Mt. 23:23)

Conflict Over the Sabbath

With this background, we are now in a position to appreciate Jesus' Sabbath controversy with the Pharisees in Mark 2:23–3:6. Throughout his Gospel, Mark presents a compelling picture of Jesus as the Messiah appointed to lead Israel out of exile. In the course of his presentation, Mark gives a series of vignettes in which Jesus vindicates His ministry despite increasing opposition from the scribes and Pharisees (2:1–3:6). First, the scribes internally question Jesus' righteousness after Jesus forgives the sins of the paralytic. Next, the Pharisees question His disciples about their Master's association with sinners and tax collectors. Third, the disciples of John and of the Pharisees ask Jesus why His disciples aren't fasting for the return from exile. In each conflict, Jesus vindicates Himself by pointing out His unique identity—He is the Son of Man who has authority to forgive sins; He is the Great Physician who has come to heal the sick; He is the Bridegroom in whose presence feasting, and not fasting, is fitting.[1]

This pattern of conflict followed by vindication culminates in two more stories that both revolve around the same topic—the Sabbath. Although Mark describes what a typical Sabbath day looked like in the life of our Lord earlier in his Gospel (1:21–39),[2] he now reveals that Jesus' observance of the Sabbath didn't quite fit the Pharisees' notion of what was acceptable. Because Jesus didn't meet their expectations, conflict ensues once again.

> [23]Now it happened that [Jesus] went through the grain-fields on the Sabbath; and as they went His disciples began to pluck the heads of grain. [24]And the Pharisees said to Him, "Look, why do they do what is not lawful on the Sabbath?"
>
> [25]But He said to them, "Have you never read what David did when he was in need and hungry, he and those with him: [26]how he went into the house of God in the days of Abiathar the high priest, and ate the showbread, which is not lawful to eat except for the priests, and also gave some to those who were with him?"

---

[1]All these titles are based on the Old Testament: Son of Man (cf. Dan. 7:13ff with 9:24ff); Great Physician (cf. Jer. 8:21–22 with Is. 53:4–6); Bridegroom (cf. Is. 62:1–5).

[2]The next chapter will highlight the significance of this passage for our own observance of the Lord's Day.

> [27]And He said to them, "The Sabbath was made for man, and not man for the Sabbath. [28]Therefore the Son of Man is also Lord of the Sabbath."
>
> [1]And He entered the synagogue again, and a man was there who had a withered hand. [2]So they watched Him closely, whether He would heal him on the Sabbath, so that they might accuse Him. [3]And He said to the man who had the withered hand, "Step forward." [4]Then He said to them, "Is it lawful on the Sabbath to do good or to do evil, to save life or to kill?" But they kept silent. [5]And when He had looked around at them with anger, being grieved by the hardness of their hearts, He said to the man, "Stretch out your hand." And he stretched it out, and his hand was restored as whole as the other. [6]Then the Pharisees went out and immediately plotted with the Herodians against Him, how they might destroy Him. (Mk. 2:23–3:6)

As with the previous narrative, these two stories highlight the authority of Jesus as the Son of Man (cf. 1:22, 27; 2:10) and vindicate His authority over that of the scribes and Pharisees. Jesus is the leader of Israel whom we should follow. How do we know this is the case? Because in the same way that Jesus vindicated His authority to forgive sins by healing the paralytic, He now vindicates His authority to regulate the Sabbath by healing the man with the withered hand.

The controversy begins when the disciples pluck heads of grain while walking through a field, an action specifically permitted by the law as a visible testimony that all the land belonged to Yahweh (cf. Deut. 23:25). Therefore, the problem was not what they were doing, but rather when—on the Sabbath, possibly while traveling to reach the synagogue mentioned in 3:1. Their action prompts the accusatory question of the Pharisees: "Look, why do they do what is not lawful on the Sabbath?"

Technically speaking, the law did not forbid this action on the Sabbath. Nevertheless, Jewish tradition classified what they did as reaping—which was specifically forbidden (cf. Exod. 34:21). For the moment, Jesus assumes the legitimacy of their interpretation and demonstrates that even if it were correct, He and His disciples would be justified.

The Son of David

Jesus begins by asking them an ironic question: "Have you never read . . . ?" Of course, as He begins to relate the story, it is clear that the Pharisees would have read the passage. After all, the story of David's flight from Saul was, and still is, one of the most well-known stories in the Old Testament. Yet Jesus' question reveals that on a very fundamental level they have failed to read it, because they are unable to apply it correctly to the question they are asking.

Note also that Jesus does not claim to be free from the constraints of God's law. Rather, He highlights the Pharisees' shallow reading of the law and how they failed to give heed to the entire warp and woof of biblical instruction. In particular, Jesus demonstrates how their application failed to understand His identity. He does this by citing an incident in the life of David—subtly encouraging His audience to identify Him as David's promised heir.

In 1 Samuel 21, David—the lawfully anointed but not yet enthroned king—was being unjustly pursued by Saul and his armies and fled to the tabernacle and the priests at Nob. Hungry and in need, he requested food. None was available except the showbread which the priests placed before the altar every Sabbath and which they were permitted to eat once it had served its sacred function. The high priest gave David some of the bread, and David and his men ate it. The problem, as Jesus points out, is that this wasn't technically lawful.

According to Leviticus 24:9, the showbread was "most holy" and was, therefore, only to be eaten by the priests.

> And [the showbread] shall be for Aaron and his sons, and they shall eat it in a holy place; for it is most holy to him from the offerings of the LORD made by fire, by a perpetual statute.

The bread was for Aaron and his sons—not for the commoners, not for the kings—and was to be eaten in a holy place. Nevertheless, David is not condemned for eating the showbread in 1 Samuel. Indeed, he is presented as the righteous party while Doeg the Edomite, David's betrayer, is condemned as the wicked one. David ate the showbread righteously. But it wasn't technically lawful. How do we understand this apparent discrepancy?

Many advocates of the perpetuity of the Sabbath have argued that at this point, Jesus is articulating the principle that "works of necessity" are permitted on the Sabbath. According to this view David was "in need and hungry," which means that he was permitted to violate the law because of his extreme circumstances. It is difficult to see the plausibility of this argument, however. While the example of David can be interpreted as a case of dire necessity, the case of Jesus' disciples cannot. The disciples were, after all, in the midst of Israel, and hospitality customs would have dictated that they be fed if in need. Further, even had they not been fed, they could have survived another day without getting those heads of grain.

What is the parallel between the actions of Jesus and his disciples and the actions of David and his men? The parallel has to do with Jesus' identity as David's heir. David ate the bread righteously because, as the Lord's Anointed, his calling to set up his kingdom was more important than the restriction against eating the showbread. David had divine work to do and this work took precedence over the showbread restriction.

And so, Jesus implies, the same thing is going on with Him and His disciples.

Already Mark has revealed that Jesus has been traveling to the various villages of Galilee in order to preach the arrival of the Kingdom of God (cf. 1:14–15, 39). Now Jesus is saying, "As we're traveling around doing this Kingdom work, the disciples are getting hungry and we've got a job to do. Just like in David's day, this Kingdom work takes precedence over lesser matters of the law, over the Sabbath itself. We've got work to do; we're fishers of men; we're calling people into the kingdom. Consequently, it is fitting for Me and My disciples to put aside the lesser matters of the law in order to attend to My calling as the Anointed, as the Messiah."

The fundamental problem of the Pharisees, in other words, was not their application of the Sabbath law, but their failure to grasp the identity of Jesus. If they really understood who he was—that He was the Son of David come to establish His Kingdom—then they would have put these questions in their proper perspective. But since they missed that, their handling of the Sabbath gets bungled as well.

Lord of the Sabbath

But how do we know that the Sabbath is a "lesser matter"? Jesus' analogy only works if the Sabbath is somewhat similar to the restriction on the showbread. But the Sabbath command, we can imagine the Pharisees protesting, was included among the Ten Commandments. So how does Jesus justify the parallel between the Sabbath and the restriction of the showbread? He justifies it by going back to the creation of the Sabbath—similar to what he does later in the Gospel with marriage and divorce (cf. Mk. 10:5ff).

> [27]And He said to them, "The Sabbath was made for man, and not man for the Sabbath. [28]Therefore the Son of Man is also Lord of the Sabbath." (Mk. 2:27–28)

When God created the Sabbath, Jesus states, He created it for the benefit of man—not the other way around. Fundamentally, Jesus says, rest every seventh day was given to refresh and restore, not to confine and restrict. As we saw earlier, the Sabbath embodied principles of justice and equity, forbidding exploitation of the poorest members of society. Sabbath was Jubilee—freedom from slavery, freedom from debt, freedom from labor, rest in the presence of God.

> Six days you shall do your work, and on the seventh day you shall rest, *that your ox and your donkey may rest, and the son of your female servant and the stranger may be refreshed.* (Exod. 23:12 cf. Deut. 5:12–15)

To pull a point from the last chapter, Jesus clearly categorizes the Sabbath as positive law—law introduced not so much because it inherently reflects the character of God but rather because it expresses His will. In particular, the Sabbath expressed God's desire for man's rest and refreshment: for liberty, joy, health, fullness, happiness, growth. Consequently, the things done on the Sabbath should be things that promote life, promote well being, and advance the joy and happiness of men while upholding the honor and worship of God. The Sabbath was created for the benefit of man and, consequently, served a subservient role to man's well being. And what more fully promotes man's well being than to be enrolled in the Kingdom of God? To be restored to fellowship with God and the land?

Isaiah describes the work that will be accomplished by the Servant of the Lord, and he describes the work in terms of liberation, freedom, and joy.

6"I, the Lord, have called You in righteousness,
And will hold Your hand;
I will keep You and give You as a covenant to the people,
As a light to the Gentiles,
7To open blind eyes,
To bring out prisoners from the prison,
Those who sit in darkness from the prison house."
(Is. 42:6–7)

Sing, O heavens!
Be joyful, O earth!
And break out in singing, O mountains!
For the Lord has comforted His people,
And will have mercy on His afflicted. (Is. 49:13)

"The Spirit of the Lord God is upon Me,
Because the Lord has anointed Me
To preach good tidings to the poor;
He has sent Me to heal the brokenhearted,
To proclaim liberty to the captives,
And the opening of the prison to those who are bound."
(Is. 61:1)

Jeremiah evokes imagery of rest to describe the coming rescue
from exile under the leadership of the Davidic heir:

8"For it shall come to pass in that day,"
Says the LORD of hosts,
"That I will break his yoke from your neck,
And will burst your bonds;
Foreigners shall no more enslave them.
9But they shall serve the LORD their God,
And David their king,
Whom I will raise up for them.
10"Therefore do not fear, O My servant Jacob," says the LORD,
"Nor be dismayed, O Israel;
For behold, I will save you from afar,

And your seed from the land of their captivity.
Jacob shall return, have rest and be quiet,
And no one shall make him afraid." (Jer. 30:8–10)

In other words, the Servant's work would embody the principles that were embedded within the Sabbath. His work was Sabbath. "Come to Me, all you who labor and are heavy laden, and I will give you rest" (Mt. 11:28). The Son of Man—the one who represents God on earth and is appointed to bring in the rule of God, the Son of David who is going about setting up His Kingdom—is Lord even of the Sabbath. His work is of far greater significance than the Sabbath itself. He, like His father David before Him, is fully justified in His conduct because Kingdom work is of far greater importance, of far greater weight, than the Sabbath itself.[3]

What we see then is that this first vignette recorded by Mark is no mere moralistic manifesto asserting that works of necessity are lawful on the Sabbath. Like the three previous conflicts, Jesus' answer to the Pharisees' question is tied intimately to His Person. Not only is He the Son of Man who has authority to forgive sins; not only is He the Great Physician who heals sinners; not only is He the Bridegroom come to wed His bride; He is also the Son of David come to establish His Kingdom.[4]

---

[3]None of this should be taken to imply that Jesus agreed with the Pharisees' interpretation of the Sabbath. See the discussion below.

[4]This story thus has ramifications for the interpretation of Hebrews 4:1–10. In Jesus we enter into the Sabbath perpetually and are thus enabled to celebrate the Christian Sabbath, the Lord's Day, more fully than our Old Testament fathers ever could (cf. Heb. 11:39–40).

Is It Lawful on the Sabbath?

This brings us to the second part of the Sabbath conflict. Here we learn that not only is Jesus Lord of the Sabbath in the sense that His Kingdom work takes precedence over the Sabbath itself, He is also Lord of the Sabbath in the sense that He is its definitive interpreter and applier. As the Son of Man, He is the one with the authority to determine what is lawful or not on this day.

In the first story, Jesus demonstrated that even if the Pharisees' interpretation of Sabbath law was valid, His actions were justified because His work as the Son of David embodied the very principles enshrined in the Sabbath. In the second, however, He boldly attacks their position and reveals its folly and triviality. He undermines their whole method of interpretation and demonstrates that they have misconstrued the nature of the Sabbath.

Jesus, entering the synagogue on the Sabbath as the Lord of the Sabbath, sees a man in the assembly with a withered hand. He knows that the Pharisees are eager to judge Him, and so He challenges them with a question about the nature of the day: "Is it lawful on the Sabbath to do good or to do evil, to save life or to kill?" (Mk. 3:1–4).

Given what we have learned about the Sabbath thus far, we should know the answer to this question. Remember what we discovered earlier about the principles embodied in the Sabbath. How did Isaiah define Sabbath keeping (cf. Is. 56:1–2)? Keeping justice; preserving life; preventing exploitation. And here is a man in need of healing—is not the Sabbath the most fitting day for his deliverance? Of course! As Matthew records Jesus speaking on this occasion,

> [11]"What man is there among you who has one sheep, and if it falls into a pit on the Sabbath, will not lay hold of it and

lift it out? [12]Of how much more value then is a man than a sheep? Therefore it is lawful to do good on the Sabbath. (Mt. 12:11–12)

But the tradition of the elders disagreed. While it conceded that life-threatening illnesses could be healed on the Sabbath, all other illnesses were to be treated on other days (cf. Lk. 13:14). Healing, after all, is a type of work, and work was forbidden on the Sabbath.

Jesus undermines this entire process of reasoning by framing his question to highlight what is lawful on the Sabbath, not what is unlawful. *"Is it lawful on the Sabbath* to do good or to do evil, to save life or to kill?"* His question forces them to consider why God created the Sabbath and brings us back to His previous answer: the Sabbath was made for man.

The Pharisees' approach to the Sabbath, rather than imitating the Creator and Redeemer, imitated the Serpent in the garden. God had commanded Adam, "Of every tree of the garden you may freely eat; but of the tree of the knowledge of good and evil you shall not eat, for in the day that you eat of it you shall surely die" (Gen. 2:16–17). We see that the original prohibition from the tree of the knowledge of good and evil was given in the context of vast liberality. Adam was free to eat from all the trees in the garden—a startling array of colors and flavors lay before him. To deceive our first parents, however, the Serpent focuses upon the restriction rather than the liberality. "Has God indeed said, 'You shall not eat of every tree of the garden?'" (Gen. 3:1). If we compare this with the way the Pharisees approached the Sabbath, we notice a striking similarity. Rather than revel in the life-giving, liberating joy of the Sabbath, the Pharisees turned it into a set of shackles. Jesus rebukes them for this folly and insists that "the Sabbath was made for man, not man for the Sabbath" (Mk. 2:27). The Sabbath was not made to oppress or to destroy but to liberate.

The Pharisees, however, are unwilling to think in these terms. They have already decided against Jesus. He is not supporting their vision of the Kingdom; He is not supporting their interpretation and application of the Sabbath law; He is setting Himself up as an independent source of knowledge and light. Consequently, they are no longer interested in hearing—only in justifying their opposition and looking for an opportunity to "accuse Him" (Mk. 3:2).

Jesus obliges. He is not frightened by their opposition. Rather, He is angered by their hypocrisy and grieved by their hardness of heart. Here is a man, a son of Abraham even, who is in bondage; yet, those who are supposedly zealous for the law are unwilling to help him. So Jesus speaks and restores the man's hand. Immediately, the Pharisees respond—not in wonder (Mk. 1:27–28) or admiration (2:12), but with deadly opposition. "Then the Pharisees went out and immediately plotted with the Herodians against Him, how they might destroy him" (Mk. 3:6). Apparently they have decided that it is more righteous to do evil on the Sabbath rather than good, to destroy life rather than save it.

Conclusion

We return then to our opening story about Rollo and Charles the Simple. Rollo preserved the custom of paying homage but turned it on its head by failing to uphold the principle embodied in it. Likewise, the scribes and Pharisees were observing the Sabbath in such a way that they totally missed why the Sabbath had been created. God made it for the benefit of man, to grant him joy and refreshment in the presence of his loving and wise Creator, but the scribes and Pharisees had turned it into a burden. They used the law to enslave rather than to liberate. But Jesus, as the Son of Man, comes to set the captives free and return them to the glorious liberty of Sabbath observance. He upholds not only the ceremony, but also the principles behind it, and so makes the Sabbath a delight (cf. Is. 58:13–14).

CHAPTER 4

A Typical Sabbath Day

Introduction

Charles Sheldon, a Congregationalist minister in Topeka, Kansas, in the late 1800s, is best known for his novel *In His Steps*. The main protagonist in the story, Rev. Henry Maxwell, finds his ministry challenged and transformed by a homeless man:

> I heard some people singing at a church prayer meeting the other night,
>
> > "All for Jesus, all for Jesus,
> > All my being's ransomed powers,
> > All my thoughts, and all my doings,
> > All my days, and all my hours."
>
> and I kept wondering as I sat on the steps outside just what they meant by it. It seems to me there's an awful lot of trouble in the world that somehow wouldn't exist if all the people

who sing such songs went and lived them out. I suppose I don't understand. But what would Jesus do? Is that what you mean by following His steps? It seems to me sometimes as if the people in the big churches had good clothes and nice houses to live in, and money to spend for luxuries, and could go away on summer vacations and all that, while the people outside the churches, thousands of them, I mean, die in tenements, and walk the streets for jobs, and never have a piano or a picture in the house, and grow up in misery and drunkenness and sin.

Challenged by the man's words and convicted by the man's death in his home a short time later, Maxwell and his congregation vowed to live like Jesus for the next year, doing nothing without first asking themselves, "What would Jesus do?" As a result their town was transformed—unemployment dropped, housing improved, schools were started. Rumor of these changes soon spread to other cities which likewise reaped the fruit of such reflection.

Sheldon's book struck a chord with American Christians and became a runaway bestseller. To date it is the thirty-ninth best-selling book of all time. The enduring impact of his work was witnessed in the 1990s, one hundred years after its publication, with the manufacture of millions of WWJD trinkets.

While many of Sheldon's exhortations reflect the pietistic notions of his day—opposing all use of alcohol, speaking negatively of God-given wealth, and so on—the central question is a good one, and it's one which Christians throughout the ages have continually asked: what would Jesus do?

So, for our purposes, let's make this question more specific: what would Jesus do on the Lord's Day were He here with us today?

Imitate Christ

This question is relevant because the New Testament insists that the basic vision for Christian obedience is to become like Jesus, to reflect His character in our own and His life in our own. In the Gospel of Mark, Jesus remarks:

> [42]You know that those who are considered rulers over the Gentiles lord it over them, and their great ones exercise authority over them. [43]Yet it shall not be so among you; but whoever desires to become great among you shall be your servant. [44]And whoever of you desires to be first shall be slave of all. [45]*For even the Son of Man did not come to be served, but to serve,* and to give His life a ransom for many. (Mk. 10:42–45)

Our pattern for life is the life of Christ. And so the rest of the Scriptures constantly direct us back to the example of Jesus to regulate our conduct. "Imitate me," Paul urges the Corinthians, "just as I also imitate Christ" (1 Cor. 11:1). Likewise Peter commands servants to be submissive to their masters, "For to this you were called, because Christ also suffered for us, leaving us an example, that you should follow His steps" (1 Pet. 2:21). And later, he exhorts all his readers, "Therefore, since Christ suffered for us in the flesh, arm yourselves also with the same mind" (1 Pet. 4:1). Imitation is the essence of discipleship. As we worship and serve the Lord, we become more like him. "But we all, with unveiled face, beholding as in a mirror the glory of the Lord, are being transformed into the same image from glory to glory, just as by the Spirit of the Lord" (2 Cor. 3:18).

This principle is nothing new. After all, we saw it reflected in the giving of the Sabbath regulations in the Old Testament. Why were the people of God to rest? Because the Creator rested on the seventh day and blessed it (cf. Exod. 20:11). Why were the Israelites to grant rest to those under their charge, their servants, children, and livestock? Because God granted them rest in rescuing them from Egypt (cf. Deut. 5:15).

A Typical Sabbath Day

As we seek to flesh out what our observance of the Lord's Day should look like, we should begin by asking what Scripture tells us of Jesus' life on the Sabbath. Typically, those who look to the Gospels for such information turn immediately to Jesus' controversy with the Pharisees (which we considered in the last chapter). These passages are certainly helpful: at the very least, they reveal that Jesus' approach differed markedly from that of the scribes and Pharisees. In addition, these conflicts highlight Jesus' way of directing His hearers to think positively—to think first and foremost of what we can do on the Sabbath rather than what we can't.

On one level, therefore, it is helpful to formulate a vision for the Lord's Day by going directly to Jesus' Sabbath controversy with the scribes and Pharisees. These passages are clearly about the Sabbath and Jesus is correcting grave misconceptions about the nature of the day. However, our tendency to jump immediately to these passages can cause us to overlook others. For there are other texts which more subtly, and yet powerfully, reveal Jesus' approach to the Sabbath and furnish us with a pattern to imitate.

Consider, for example, Mark's opening presentation of Jesus' ministry. Jesus has just announced the fulfillment of God's promises of redemption and the coming of the Kingdom of God in His person (1:14–15). He has also called a number of men to join Him as disciples, or students (1:16–20). Now Jesus proceeds to carry on His ministry of "fishing for men" in the land of Israel.[1]

[1] For the metaphor of "fishers of men" connected with the return from exile, the promise of redemption, see Jeremiah 16:14-16.

²¹Then they went into Capernaum, and immediately on the Sabbath [Jesus] entered the synagogue and taught. ²²And they were astonished at His teaching, for He taught them as one having authority, and not as the scribes.

²³Now there was a man in their synagogue with an unclean spirit. And he cried out, ²⁴saying, "Let us alone! What have we to do with You, Jesus of Nazareth? Did You come to destroy us? I know who You are—the Holy One of God!"

²⁵But Jesus rebuked him, saying, "Be quiet, and come out of him!" ²⁶And when the unclean spirit had convulsed him and cried out with a loud voice, he came out of him. ²⁷Then they were all amazed, so that they questioned among themselves, saying, "What is this? What new doctrine is this? For with authority He commands even the unclean spirits, and they obey Him." ²⁸And immediately His fame spread throughout all the region around Galilee.

²⁹Now as soon as they had come out of the synagogue, they entered the house of Simon and Andrew, with James and John. ³⁰But Simon's wife's mother lay sick with a fever, and they told Him about her at once. ³¹So He came and took her by the hand and lifted her up, and immediately the fever left her. And she served them.

³²At evening, when the sun had set, they brought to Him all who were sick and those who were demon-possessed. ³³And the whole city was gathered together at the door. ³⁴Then He healed many who were sick with various diseases, and cast out many demons; and He did not allow the demons to speak, because they knew Him.

³⁵Now in the morning, having risen a long while before daylight, He went out and departed to a solitary place; and there He prayed. ³⁶And Simon and those who were with Him searched for Him. ³⁷When they found Him, they said to Him, "Everyone is looking for You."

³⁸But He said to them, "Let us go into the next towns, that I may preach there also, because for this purpose I have come forth."

³⁹And He was preaching in their synagogues throughout all Galilee, and casting out demons. (Mk. 1:21–39)

Here Mark is describing a typical Sabbath day in the life of our Lord. In verse 21 we are told that Jesus was in Capernaum and that he entered into the synagogue "on the Sabbath." This time indicator governs the rest of the section. After all, verse 29 tells us that "as soon as they had come out of the synagogue," Jesus entered into the house of Simon and Andrew along with James and John. Then, on the evening of the same day (v. 32), "once the sun had set," all kinds of other folks were brought to Jesus that He might heal them and deliver them from demons. Clearly Mark is giving us a summary of a Sabbath day in Jesus' life.

It seems that Mark intends this summary to govern our understanding of what Jesus usually did on the Sabbath. In verse 35 we are told that the next morning Jesus went out to a solitary place away from Capernaum in order to pray. When His disciples finally found Him, they encouraged Him to return to Capernaum. "But He said to them, 'Let us go into the next towns, that I may preach there also, because for this purpose I have come forth'" (v. 38). Jesus refused to return to Capernaum so that He could go and repeat what He had done in Capernaum in the other villages of Israel. And this is precisely what Jesus did. "And He was preaching in their synagogues throughout all Galilee, and casting out demons" (v. 39). Mark tells us that Jesus was preaching in their synagogues regularly. When would He have done this? *On the Sabbath.*

Mark, therefore, is describing a typical Sabbath day in the life of our Lord. He provides us with a concrete description of Jesus' Sabbath life so that we can meditate upon it and take it as a pattern for our own observance of the Lord's Day. The delightful thing is that Mark gives us a vision for the entire day, beginning with corporate worship and extending to works of mercy and necessity as well as fellowship. In this chapter, let us consider what the life of Jesus tells us about the Sabbath and corporate worship.

Corporate Worship

The first thing we observe in this passage is that Jesus gathered together publicly with the people of God for worship. "Then they went into Capernaum, and immediately on the Sabbath He entered into the synagogue" (v. 21). Jesus recognized the centrality of corporate worship for His life as Messiah. He did not exhibit a "Me and My Father Alone" ministry. While spending time alone with God was a priority in Jesus' life (cf. Mk. 1:35), it was no substitute for the corporate worship which was characteristic of both Jesus' ministry and His early life. "So [Jesus] came to Nazareth, where He had been brought up. *And as His custom was,* He went into the synagogue on the Sabbath day, and stood up to read" (Lk. 4:16). As a good Jew, as one who was born "under the law" (cf. Gal. 4:4) and who did all things, to please His Father, Jesus participated in the public worship of Israel throughout His life.

In the time of Jesus, weekly corporate worship was manifest in Israel in local assemblies called "synagogues," a transliteration of the Greek word *synagōgē* (literally, "a bringing together"). The foundation of the synagogue system is laid out in Leviticus 23:3, where the observance of the weekly Sabbath was mandated in all the various villages of Israel:

> Six days shall work be done, but the seventh day is a Sabbath of solemn rest, a holy convocation. You shall do no work on it; it is the Sabbath of the Lord in all your dwellings.

Note that the Sabbath was a "holy convocation," a gathering together of the people of God in all their various villages.

While worship at the central sanctuary in Jerusalem occurred three times each year (cf. Lev. 23:4ff) and while private worship could happen whenever, corporate worship was celebrated weekly on the Sabbath.[2] God commanded this and Jesus observed it.

This harmonizes well with what we learned about the abiding validity of the Sabbath commandment in the first chapter. The Sabbath regulates corporate worship. As we saw in our study of the Ten Commandments, the first four commandments revolve around the issue of worship: Whom are we to worship? In what manner are we to worship Him? In what way are we to worship? When are we to worship? Without a specific command from God, society is left adrift with little sense of how to structure time. God's Word makes clear that we are to structure our time as a reflection of God's activity in creation—six days of labor with one day of (corporate) worship and rest.

So, given that our calling as the people of God is to imitate our Lord and Savior Jesus, what should our Lord's Day look like? Quite simply, we need to be gathering together with the people of God for worship. Corporate worship was one of Jesus' priorities and it should be one of ours as well. It is not optional nor a mere accessory of discipleship. Rather, it is an essential part of following Jesus. The author of Hebrews makes this clear: "And let us consider one another in order to stir up love and good works, not forsaking the assembling of ourselves together, as is the manner of some, but exhorting one another, and so much the more as you see the Day approaching" (Heb. 10:24–25).

Since Jesus considered corporate worship a necessity for His spiritual development and growth, can we really claim to

---

[2] For the connection between the synagogues of Jesus' day and Leviticus 23:3, see James B. Jordan, *Through New Eyes: Developing a Biblical View of the World* (Eugene: Wipf and Stock Publishers, 1999), 202–204.

be able to survive on less? He who enjoyed a perfect relationship with His Heavenly Father nevertheless felt it was critical to attend the public gatherings of the people of God. On the Sabbath, He did not retreat into a cave like a hermit. He did not go out and meditate on the hills overlooking the beautiful Judean countryside. He went to the synagogue and worshiped with God's people.

Notice also that Jesus' action undermines our complaint against the quality of the churches in our area. Frequently we try to excuse ourselves from corporate worship by claiming that there simply aren't any good churches to attend. But here's where the text slaps us in the face. How long has it been since you entered a church and ran into a demon possessed man? I dare say that if your experience is like mine it has never happened. Yet this was the state of the synagogues in Jesus' day—and He still made a priority of meeting with these folks. The Sinless One made a priority of gathering with hypocritical sinners for worship. It follows that corporate worship should characterize our Lord's Day.

Teaching on the Lord's Day

But let us press further in our study of this typical Sabbath day. Why is it that corporate worship is so important? Fortunately, Mark does not leave us guessing. His narrative reveals two reasons why gathering with God's people for worship is imperative: when we worship, we hear the very voice of God in the teaching of His Word and we wage war against His enemies.

Consider first the centrality of teaching in corporate worship. As a society, Israel was oriented around the Word of God. It was the custom in the synagogues each Sabbath to read portions from the Old Testament Scriptures and then to invite a rabbi or teacher to comment upon the text. Whereas other cultures were oriented around images or idols as the means of communing and communicating with their deity, Israel was oriented around the Word. When the Israelites met Yahweh at Mount Sinai, they saw no shape or form; they only heard His voice. Consequently, Israel was to orient herself around the life-giving Word of her God (cf. Deut. 4:1–40), not dead and lifeless idols (cf. Ps. 115:1–11).

As a young man, Jesus studied and grew in His comprehension and grasp of the Word of God. This included saturated enculturation while in Joseph and Mary's home (cf. Lk. 2:51–52; Deut. 6:1ff), occasional notable conversations at the temple (cf. Lk. 2:41–50), and routine exposure to the Scriptures every Sabbath at the synagogue (cf. Lk. 4:16). As the Servant of the Lord, Jesus was a faithful student of God's Word:

> [4]The Lord GOD has given Me
> The tongue of the learned,
> That I should know how to speak
> A word in season to him who is weary.
> He awakens Me morning by morning,
> He awakens My ear
> To hear as the learned.
> [5]The Lord GOD has opened My ear;
> And I was not rebellious,
> Nor did I turn away. (Is. 50:4–5)

Jesus sat in the synagogue, listening to the reading of the Scriptures and to the explanation offered by the rabbis—no doubt disagreeing privately with their interpretations at times but always listening to the voice of God in the Word.

In the text from Mark, however, Jesus is no longer the disciple; He is the teacher. Consequently, when He enters the synagogue, He teaches. He reads the appointed text and explains its significance now that the Kingdom of God has arrived in Him (cf. Lk. 4:16ff). And His message causes quite a stir. For here is One who speaks from the Word with the very voice of God, with a voice of authority (cf. Mk. 1:22). Those who have ears to hear listen and are amazed.

Teaching is a central Sabbath theme throughout the New Testament. Like Jesus, we must saturate ourselves in the Word of God on the Lord's Day, listening as it is read and preached during corporate worship. For example, Paul exhorts Timothy as a minister in the church at Ephesus, "Until I come, give attention to the public reading of Scripture, to exhortation and teaching" (1 Tim. 4:13, NASB). Later Paul exhorts him again, "Preach the word! Be ready in season and out of season. Convince, rebuke, exhort, with all longsuffering and teaching" (2 Tim. 4:2). Similarly, John pronounces a blessing on "he who reads and those who hear the words of this prophecy" (Rev. 1:3). John's words reveal the same basic pattern as synagogue worship where the Scriptures were read and then explained by those who were trained. Clearly, the Apostles believed that public attention to Scripture—its reading and its explanation—was as critical to the life of the Church as it was to the life of the synagogue.

And here is the exciting thing: Paul tells us that when the preacher preaches the Word of God accurately, the hearer does not simply hear about God in the sermon—he or she actually hears God Himself. "How then will they call on Him in whom they have not believed? And how will they believe in Him whom they have not heard? And how will they hear without a preacher?" (Rom. 10:14, NASB). Notice Paul's second question, "And how will they believe in Him *whom they have not heard?*" Notice that Paul doesn't say "about whom" they have not heard, but "whom" they have not heard. When the preacher preaches, the one listening does not simply hear the preacher; he hears the very voice of Christ (cf. Heb. 12:25).

So when we attend corporate worship each Lord's Day, we do so that we might hear from God Himself, hear Him speak to our current situation, hear Him uncover our sin, hear Him comfort us in our sorrow. "For the word of God is living and powerful, and sharper than any two-edged sword, piercing even to the division of soul and spirit, and of joints and marrow, and is a discerner of the thoughts and intents of the heart" (Heb. 4:12). It was not only during Jesus' earthly ministry that He taught in the synagogues of Israel. He continues to do so through the preaching of His Word and the work of His Spirit every Lord's Day in our pulpits. Who would want to miss that?

The Battle is the Lord's

But teaching is not the only activity in which our Lord engages during this typical Sabbath worship service. He also goes to war with His enemies. Jesus enters the synagogue and a man with an unclean spirit berates Him and challenges Him. "Let us alone! What have we to do with You, Jesus of Nazareth? Did You come to destroy us? I know who You are—the Holy One of God!" (Mk. 1:24).

The existence of evil spirits or demons has been recognized in most societies and was acknowledged very early in biblical teaching. In describing Israel's rebellion in the wilderness, for example, Moses remarks:

> [16]They provoked Him to jealousy with foreign gods; with abominations they provoked Him to anger. [17]They sacrificed to demons, not to God. (Deut. 32:16–17)

Throughout the Scriptures, demons are coupled with the Devil himself. Like him, demons are fallen angels who rebelled against God and refused to submit to His authority (cf. Jude 6). Prior to the coming of Christ, demons had considerable power, having secured rule over various kingdoms and nations (cf. Dan. 10:12ff). They even used their abilities to overthrow the minds and spirits of men and women foolish enough to trifle with them. Demons were and are the most resolute enemies of God, wholly devoted to the overthrow of His Kingdom.

It is no wonder, therefore, that when Jesus comes announcing the arrival of the Kingdom of God, the demons are agitated. Jesus has already gone head-to-head with Satan and resisted his temptations (Mk. 1:12–13 cf. Mt. 4:1–11). Now Jesus begins His ministry and the combined armies of the evil one gather together against Him. Once again Jesus is triumphant; the unclean spirit is defeated. "But Jesus rebuked him, saying, 'Be quiet, and come out of him!' And when the unclean spirit had convulsed him and cried out with a loud voice, he came out of him" (Mk. 1:25–26; cf. 1:32–34; 3:11–12).

The New Testament insists that these earthly battles between Jesus and the demonic forces culminated in the cross where Jesus defeated the powers of darkness. "Having disarmed principalities and powers, He made a public spectacle of them, triumphing over them in [the cross]" (Col. 2:15). The power that Satan and the demonic forces once had has been forever broken. As Hebrews declares:

> [14]Inasmuch then as the children have partaken of flesh and blood, He Himself likewise shared in the same, that through death He might destroy him who had the power of death, that is, the devil, [15]and release those who through fear of death were all their lifetime subject to bondage. (Heb. 2:14–15)

As we consider Jesus' battle with the demon in the synagogue, we might be tempted to conclude that it has little application today. After all, most of us live in post-Christianized civilizations where the prevalence of demon possession is marginal. We don't typically run into demon-possessed individuals when we enter the bars downtown, let alone the churches. So how does this story apply to Sabbath-keeping?

The answer is that through corporate worship Christ continues to go to war against His enemies every Lord's Day. Worship is warfare. When the people of God gather and worship, we wage war on the enemies of God.[3]

Consider the story of Jehoshaphat in 2 Chronicles. Jehoshaphat was a righteous king who loved the Lord and desired to honor him. During his reign the Ammonites, Moabites, and Edomites formed an alliance to destroy Judah. Jehoshaphat responded as any righteous king should—he sought the Lord in prayer and fasting, requesting God's intervention in this terrible crisis. He was assured of God's protection through the Levitical singer Jahaziel and the next day led Israel into battle, arranging the order of battle so that the Levitical choir led the army into battle.

> [21]And when he had consulted with the people, he appointed those who should sing to the LORD, and who should praise the beauty of holiness, as they went out before the army and were saying:
> "Praise the LORD,
>   For His mercy endures forever."
> [22]Now when they began to sing and to praise, the LORD set ambushes against the people of Ammon, Moab, and Mount Seir, who had come against Judah; and they were defeated. [23]For the people of Ammon and Moab stood up against the

---

[3] This is why (1) we are commanded to sing the Psalms (cf. Eph. 5:19; Col. 3:16) and (2) so many of the psalms speak of "enemies" (e.g., Ps. 3:7; 5:8; 6:7,10; 7:6; 8:2; etc.). This is also why the imprecatory psalms, the psalms calling down curses upon the enemies of God, are important for us to sing. By singing them, we call upon God to go to war against His enemies —to conquer them by converting them (cf. Ps. 83:16) or destroying them (cf. Ps. 137). For an excellent treatment of this theme, see James E. Adams, *War Psalms of the Prince of Peace: Lessons from the Imprecatory Psalms* (Phillipsburg: P&R, 1991).

inhabitants of Mount Seir to utterly kill and destroy them. And when they had made an end of the inhabitants of Seir, they helped to destroy one another. (2 Chr. 20:21–23)

Notice that it was precisely when the choir began to sing and to praise the Lord (v. 22) that the Lord set ambushes against Israel's enemies. Worship moved God to act on behalf of His people.

Interestingly enough, this metaphor of worship as warfare is founded upon the Mosaic Law. The book of Numbers gives explicit instructions on the incorporation of music into the life of Israel.

> 9When you go to war in your land against the enemy who oppresses you, then you shall sound an alarm with the trumpets, and you will be remembered before the LORD your God, and you will be saved from your enemies. 10Also in the day of your gladness, in your appointed feasts, and at the beginning of your months, you shall blow the trumpets over your burnt offerings and over the sacrifices of your peace offerings; and they shall be a memorial for you before your God: I am the LORD your God. (Num. 10:9–10)

Note that trumpets were to be sounded on two specific occasions: when Israel went to war and when Israel celebrated great feasts (or, in other words, worship). Israel blew the trumpets so that the Lord would "remember" them and the noise of the trumpets would "be a memorial for [them] before [their] God." Worship calls upon the Giver of victory to rise up and protect His heritage. The trumpets remind God of His promises, remind Him that we are His people, remind Him to act on our behalf. And when the people of God start reminding God of these things faithfully and passionately, watch out! God remembers and acts; He goes to war against His and our enemies (cf. Exod. 2:23–25).

This close association of warfare and worship in the blowing of trumpets led Israel to the conclusion that worship is warfare. It reminds us that the battle is the Lord's. Deliverance does not come by means of our great wisdom or technological know-how but through the blessing of God.

> And [Jahaziel] said, "Listen, all you of Judah and you inhabitants of Jerusalem, and you, King Jehoshaphat! Thus says the LORD to you: 'Do not be afraid nor dismayed because of this great multitude, for the battle is not yours, but God's.'" (2 Chr. 20:15)

The Lord Who Sanctifies You

Bringing this back to our discussion of the centrality of worship on the Lord's Day, why do we gather for corporate worship with the people of God? Quite simply, to call God to go to battle and to be reminded by Him that the battle is not ours but His.

As we noted in our previous chapters, the Sabbath is not first and foremost imperative but indicative: that is, it is not primarily about what we are to do, but about what God has done for us. God *has created* us—and so we imitate Him. God *has redeemed* us—and so we worship Him. Resting every seventh day reminds us that the Gospel is not primarily about what we do but about what God does for us and through us.

In Exodus 31:13 God declares to Moses:

> Speak also to the children of Israel, saying: "Surely My Sabbaths you shall keep, for it is a sign between Me and you throughout your generations, *that you may know that I am the LORD who sanctifies you.*"

God insists upon this same thing in Ezekiel's pronouncements against the Judahites.

> Moreover I also gave them My Sabbaths, to be a sign between
> them and Me, *that they might know that I am the* LORD *who
> sanctifies them.* (Ezek. 20:12)

The Sabbath reminded Israel that it was the Lord who had set them apart as His own people (cf. Deut. 7:6–11) and who would continue making them more holy as they worshiped Him (cf. Deut. 10:12–22). The Sabbath was a gift to the people of Israel. It reminded them not only that God was their Creator (cf. Exod. 20:11), but that He was their Redeemer (cf. Exod. 20:2; Deut. 5:15). God was the One who saved them, who set them apart as His own special possession, choosing them from among all the nations of the earth. The Sabbath was not first and foremost law or legislation—it was Gospel, good news, glad tidings.

Knowing this helps us understand why Jesus frequently practices His work on the Sabbath. By doing so, He announces in no uncertain terms that God is delivering His people again. "In Me," Jesus is declaring, "the day of redemption has dawned; salvation has arrived."

The book of Revelation explicitly connects Lord's Day worship with the praise of God as Creator and Redeemer. John was "in the Spirit on the Lord's Day" (Rev. 1:10)—in other words, *John was granted a vision of what was really happening as the people of God began to worship Him together.* The words of praise that he heard focused on God's works of creation and redemption. The living creatures in company with the twenty-four elders bowed down and cried out:

> You are worthy, O Lord,
> To receive glory and honor and power;
> *For You created all things,*
> *And by Your will they exist and were created.* (Rev. 4:11)

And when the Lamb of God appears, the living creatures and the elders shout:

> ⁹You are worthy to take the scroll,
> And to open its seals;
> For You were slain,
> *And have redeemed us to God by Your blood*
> Out of every tribe and tongue and people and nation,
> ¹⁰And have made us kings and priests to our God;
> And we shall reign on the earth. (Rev. 5:9–10)

Every Lord's Day when we gather and worship God in the beauty of holiness, we praise Him as our Creator and worship Him as our Redeemer. We meditate on the very themes that revolve around the Sabbath throughout the Old Testament. Furthermore, as we worship, we call upon the Lord to continue Jesus' work by the power of His Spirit. "Thy Kingdom come, Thy will be done, on earth as it is in heaven" (Mt. 6:10). We worship (cf. Rev. 5:8–14) and bring our prayers before the throne of God (cf. Rev. 5:8), and God remembers us and goes to war against His enemies, vindicating His Name on the earth (cf. Rev. 6:1ff).

The biblical vision of worship, therefore, is a far cry from the sickeningly sweet drivel that is commonly called worship in the modern church. One of the reasons God's enemies have been triumphing of late is because our worship has been so namby-pamby and impotent. We have defined worship as merely "expressing emotion." But this is not the only, nor indeed the primary, definition of worship used in Scripture. Worship is an expression of love and affection (cf. Ps. 18:1ff), but it is much more. In particular, worship is warfare. And so at least some of our music should be martial in its tone. But how often do modern choruses make you want to march into battle? How often do they even call the Lord to go to battle? We should be willing, even as the Psalms are, to sing against God's enemies and call upon Him to defend His Name. "Let God arise, Let His enemies be scattered; Let those also who hate Him flee before Him" (Ps. 68:1). And this isn't just an Old Testament theme. After all, the martyrs in Revelation cry out, "How long, O Lord, holy and true, until You judge and avenge our blood on those who dwell on the earth?" (6:10). And we should sing this way precisely so that we will not be tempted to take vengeance into our own hands.

> [1]Do not keep silent, O God!
> Do not hold Your peace,
> And do not be still, O God!
> [2]For behold, Your enemies make a tumult;
> And those who hate You have lifted up their head.
> [3]They have taken crafty counsel against Your people,
> And consulted together against Your sheltered ones.
> [4]They have said, "Come, and let us cut them off from
>   being a nation,
> That the name of Israel may be remembered no more."
> (Ps. 83:1–4)

Conclusion

Thus far Mark has begun to supply us with a vision for a typical Lord's Day. It should be filled with corporate worship so that we might learn from God through His Word and ask Him to go to war against His enemies. It should be apparent that Jesus' Sabbath observance was thoroughly grounded in the Old Testament mandate that the corporate worship of God be regularized. Jesus prioritized corporate worship and, as those called to imitate our Lord and Savior in all things (cf. Col. 3:10), we must prioritize corporate worship as well. "I was glad when they said to me, 'Let us go into the house of the Lord'" (Ps. 122:1).

CHAPTER 5

Call the Sabbath a Delight

Introduction

Every family has its rituals. At age seven or eight in the Bryan household, the children sit and listen as my wife reads the complete *Little House* series by Laura Ingalls Wilder. My children love these stories, listening with rapt attention as they trace the lives of Laura and Almanzo.

One of the distinctive features of the series is its child's eye view of the Sabbath, a view that is by no means flattering. In *Little House in the Big Woods,* for example, the child Laura reveals that she hated Sundays because they were so dull. Restrictions on play were myriad—no loud playing with dolls, no stitching new clothes, no making new paper dolls. One Sunday afternoon, Laura's passions get the better of her, and she cries out in frustration, "I hate Sunday!"[1]

[1] *Little House in the Big Woods* (New York: HarperTrophy, [1932] 2004), 86.

Laura wasn't punished for this outburst. Instead, her father took her aside and told her a story about his father and his father's two brothers. On the Sundays of their childhood, they were not allowed to "joke or laugh, or even smile" but were forced to sit still upon a hard, wooden bench and study their catechism all day.

On one particular occasion, the three brothers had been tirelessly working all week on a new sled. It was winter and the hill in front of their home was perfect for sledding. Unfortunately, they were unable to finish the sled until just before dark on Saturday evening, which meant no sledding until Monday, since they "could not slide downhill [on Sunday]. That would be breaking the Sabbath." But the temptation proved too much. When their father fell asleep Sunday afternoon, the boys tiptoed out of the house, determined to try the sled out just once.

But as they slid down the hillside, going faster and faster and being careful not to make a peep, a pig suddenly emerged from the forest onto their path. Before the boys could maneuver, they slid under the pig and went racing past the house with the pig on the front of the sled, now squealing for its life. And as they looked toward their home, the image of their father standing in the doorway, observing their escapade, was forever etched in their minds. Thoroughly defeated, the boys trudged into the home and, when the Sabbath was over, received a thorough lashing from their father—who wouldn't spank them on the Sabbath since that would be work.

It's hard to tell if the story made Laura grateful for her relatively "free" Sundays. The next morning she reflected that it "was Monday morning, and Sunday would not come again for a whole week." And little Laura breathed a sigh of relief.

Inevitably, discussions of the relationship between the Lord's Day and the Sabbath reach the point of application. What should the day look like? What types of things should we do? What should we avoid? Thankfully, the Word of God is not silent on these matters. However, we do not approach this issue in a cultural vacuum. Many answers have been given to these questions in the past and so it is necessary to clear away some debris. In the process, we should get a clearer vision for the day.

Eat the Fat

As the humorous story of *Little House in the Big Woods* illustrates, those who advertise themselves as the greatest friends of the Lord's Day are frequently its worst enemies. The Pharisees were among these folks. Rather than embody the Sabbath in a way that highlighted its glory and life-giving vitality, the Pharisees trivialized it and used it to enslave others to their own strictures of conscience. It is this very ditch that Sabbatarians have fallen into time and again. No play on the Sabbath; no sledding on the Sabbath; no smiling on the Sabbath; all must be serious.

Why is this such a persistent error? One reason is that we approach the Sabbath under the guise of a fast rather than a feast. We get out our starched shirts, button them tight around our necks, and revel in the scratches that develop around our thorax. We view the Sabbath as the denial of pleasures that we enjoy other days of the week. But this is the wrong metaphor. The Old Testament presents the Sabbath not as a fast but as a feast.

Consider, for example, the description of Israel's various feasts in Leviticus 23. It begins with God's announcement to Moses: "And the Lord spoke to Moses, saying, 'Speak to the children of Israel, and say to them: "The feasts of the Lord, which you shall proclaim to be holy convocations, these are My feasts"'" (vv. 1–2). The first of the feasts which the Lord announces to Moses *is the weekly Sabbath* (v. 3). What follows is a discussion of the three annual feasts in Israel—Passover, Pentecost, and Tabernacles—along with other subsidiary celebrations. The Sabbath was to be a local, routine feast of celebration, mirroring the joyous festivity of the annual celebrations in Jerusalem.

Biblically, therefore, the Sabbath is a gift, not a burden. When the Israelites were enslaved in Egypt, they did not have the privilege of resting. It wasn't that the Sabbath hadn't been a requirement during the time of enslavement in Egypt; it was that they were slaves and didn't have the liberty to enjoy the rest. They were worked relentlessly (cf. Exod. 1:13–14). So when God rescued and redeemed Israel, He restored the Sabbath to them: they got to rest. However, many wanted to continue to act like slaves. Somehow they became convinced that the life they had lived in Egypt was good (cf. Num. 11:4–6). Consequently, serious retraining was necessary in the Mosaic era.[2] God showed them what it meant to live as a free people for their own good (cf. Deut. 12:28).

The festal nature of the Sabbath is confirmed when we read the prophets. One of the judgments threatened against disobedient Israel was the loss of the Sabbath. "I will also cause all her mirth to cease, Her feast days, Her New Moons, Her Sabbaths— All her appointed feasts" (Hos. 2:11). When God fulfilled these

[2]This helps us to understand the story in Numbers 15:30–36 concerning the man who gathered sticks on the Sabbath. God is in the midst of providing for His people. Every day he provides manna for them from heaven and, on the sixth day, provides a double portion so that the people can rest on the Sabbath. Already He has rebuked them for going out on the Sabbath to gather more manna (cf. Exod. 16:22–30). But now this man rejects the restriction that God has laid down. He goes out intentionally to gather sticks so that he can provide food for himself (cf. 1 Kgs. 17:10–12). He rejects God's provision, believing that he can define the good life for himself. His "high-handed" despising of God's commandment receives a just recompense (cf. Heb. 2:2).

threats by conquering Jerusalem, Jeremiah lamented, "The Lord has caused the appointed feasts and Sabbaths to be forgotten in Zion" (Lam. 2:6). They lost the Sabbath, *and this was a grievous thing;* it was the loss of mirth, feasting, and rest.

The history of Israel following her return to the land of Judah after the exile helps us understand the nature of biblical feasting. At this time there was widespread ignorance of God's law. Accordingly, Ezra and Nehemiah assembled the people for the Feast of Trumpets (one of the subsidiary feasts described in Leviticus 23) in order to read the Law of Moses and to celebrate the feast. When the Israelites heard the Word, however, they began to weep and to mourn because they were convicted of their sin. Ezra and Nehemiah's response to their weeping is remarkable: they comforted the people and encouraged them to cease mourning and weeping.

> [10]Then [Ezra] said to them, "Go your way, eat the fat, drink the sweet, and send portions to those for whom nothing is prepared; for this day is holy to our Lord. Do not sorrow, for the joy of the Lord is your strength." [11]So the Levites quieted all the people, saying, "Be still, for the day is holy; do not be grieved." [12]And all the people went their way to eat and drink, to send portions and rejoice greatly, because they understood the words that were declared to them. (Neh. 8:10–12)

The mourning and sadness of Israel, appropriate at certain times, was not appropriate at this moment because Trumpets was a time for feasting, not fasting. Consequently, they ate and drank, shared with those in need, and rejoiced greatly. This same type of conduct should characterize the Sabbath. It is a feast. Therefore, our celebration of the day should exude a sense of festivity and gratitude, not cantankerousness.

A Feast of Choice Pieces

Given this fundamental orientation, we are in a position to study the rest of Mark's presentation of Jesus' Sabbath observance. Did Jesus think of the Sabbath as a feast? We will find that the answer is a robust "Yes!" After all, the Old Testament describes not only the Sabbath but also the Messianic Kingdom with festive language. Consider the beautiful picture painted by Isaiah:

> 6And in this mountain
> The Lord of hosts will make for all people
> A feast of choice pieces,
> A feast of wines on the lees,
> Of fat things full of marrow,
> Of well-refined wines on the lees.
> 7And He will destroy on this mountain
> The surface of the covering cast over all people,
> And the veil that is spread over all nations.
> 8He will swallow up death forever,
> And the Lord God will wipe away tears from all faces;
> The rebuke of His people
> He will take away from all the earth;
> For the Lord has spoken.
> 9And it will be said in that day:
> "Behold, this is our God;
> We have waited for Him, and He will save us.
> This is the Lord;
> We have waited for Him;
> We will be glad and rejoice in His salvation." (Is. 25:6–9)

The Messianic kingdom is described as an abundant, overflowing feast. No wonder then that our Lord feasted and celebrated with His disciples when He arrived. His first miracle was to turn water into wine at the wedding in Cana (cf. Jn. 2), and He bore the reproach of being a "glutton and a winebibber" (cf. Mt. 11:18–19). As He declared, the Bridegroom had arrived, and the fulfillment of God's promises was at hand (cf. Mk. 2:18ff). Therefore, unlike John the Baptizer, Jesus feasted and celebrated. One of the regular times He did this was on the Sabbath. Recall our text from the last chapter:

> [29]Now as soon as they had come out of the synagogue, they entered the house of Simon and Andrew, with James and John. [30]But Simon's wife's mother lay sick with a fever, and they told Him about her at once. [31]So He came and took her by the hand and lifted her up, and immediately the fever left her. And she served them. (Mk. 1:29–31)

Note that as soon as Jesus finished worshiping with the people of God, He went to Simon's house along with Andrew, James, and John. When they arrived, Jesus discovered that Peter's mother-in-law was sick and He healed her. Immediately after, she began to serve them—presumably with a meal. And note well the joy that must have characterized this particular meal—after all, Peter's mother-in-law had been *healed*.

Whatever else Jesus and His disciples were doing on this day, therefore—whether taking naps, discussing the events of the day and the teaching of our Lord, or asking questions and striving to learn more of Jesus (cf. Mk. 4:10, 34; Lk. 10:38–42)—the one thing we know they were doing was feasting and fellowshipping with one another.

If we combine Jesus' example of feasting with the Old Testament teaching on the Sabbath and the Messianic kingdom; and then if we throw in the astonishing news of Jesus' resurrection, it should be clear why the worship of the early Church was characterized by such joy and festivity. How could worship be anything but festive? Jude remarks that the false teachers who had infiltrated the church "are spots in your *love feasts*, while they *feast with you* without fear, serving only themselves" (v. 12, cf. 2 Pet. 2:13). Similarly, Paul's rebuke of the Corinthians for their divisive feasting reveals that their celebrations were far more robust than ours frequently are. After all, he rebukes the rich for becoming drunk and satiated while the poor were left hungry (cf. 1 Cor. 11:20–22). And the problem was not that they were feasting but that they weren't waiting for the poor to enjoy the feast. In other words, Paul does not rebuke the feasting but assumes it and encourages them to include the poor. The Lord's Day is a feast, not a fast.

How is it then that our celebration of the Lord's Day, the Christian Sabbath, has frequently been so sour? Rather than hear the complaint, "Oh no! Is the Lord's Day over already?" we hear, "Oh no! It's not Sunday again, is it?" Our children, like Laura, dread the Lord's Day. But do they dread Christmas? Do they dread Easter? Do they dread birthday parties? Our children know what it is to feast; the problem is not with them—the problem is with us. We have defined the Sabbath as a fast rather than a feast, and our children's complaints simply reveal our own attitude. Jesus' action corrects this and pushes us to feast and celebrate with the people of God.

Given to Hospitality

Since the Lord's Day is a feast, what should the day look like? God has set apart this day and declared it holy. How do the Scriptures and Jesus' conduct help us fashion the day?

First, because the Lord's Day is a feast, every Lord's Day should include good food. Ideally, this would start with participation in the Lord's Supper.[3] In worship our Lord invites us to His table. He lays a banquet before us and says, "Come eat with Me. Come dine with Me" (cf. Is. 25:6–8; Rev. 3:20). He gathers us together around food and drink. He invites us to a

[3]Consult Jeffrey Meyers' excellent treatment of the contours of Lord's Day worship in *The Lord's Service* (Moscow: Canon Press, 2003).

feast—not only a feast of His Word, but a feast on His Person in the Supper.

Because our Lord invites us to a feast every Lord's Day, we learn to invite others to our feasts. Jesus, Simon, Andrew, James, John, and some of their family members feasted with one another after corporate worship. Likewise, we get to rejoice and give thanks to God together; to have our brothers and sisters into our homes; to know that in so doing we are imitating our Lord Jesus and providing a model of righteousness for the nations. "Let brotherly love continue. Do not forget to entertain strangers, for by so doing some have unwittingly entertained angels" (Heb. 13:1–2). As Paul urges us, we are to be "given to hospitality" (Rom. 12:13), and leaders in the church are to be exemplary models of this virtue (cf. 1 Tim. 3:2; 5:10; Tit. 1:8). Fellowship and feasting with the people of God gives off a pleasant aroma that draws others to the beauty of the Gospel.

Jesus' fellowship with his disciples epitomizes the shared life that reflects the very nature of God. In His prayer following the Last Supper, Jesus prayed that we would reflect the mutual sharing of the Godhead, that our fellowship with one another would image the fellowship between the Persons of the Trinity:

> [20]I do not pray for these alone, but also for those who will believe in Me through their word; [21]that they all may be one, as You, Father, are in Me, and I in You; that they also may be one in Us, that the world may believe that You sent Me. [22]And the glory which You gave Me I have given them, that they may be one just as We are one: [23]I in them, and You in Me; that they may be made perfect in one, and that the world may know that You have sent Me, and have loved them as You have loved Me. (Jn. 17:20–23)

Paul gives vent to this prayer in his many "one anothers." We are to be cherishing one another, loving one another, serving one another, giving preference to one another in love, submitting to one another in the fear of God, teaching and admonishing one another with psalms and hymns and spiritual songs. In short, we are to be fellowshipping one with another. This can only happen if we are practicing hospitality.

The Apostles were aware that practicing hospitality is at times challenging. "Oh, do we have to do it again? Do we have to cook another meal? Clean the house again?" This is especially true for the women in the congregation. While the leadership for hospitality rests with the men, the burden of hospitality usually falls most heavily upon the women. It is here that our text in Mark is so poignant. Jesus comes in and He lifts up Peter's mother-in-law. He serves her and what does she do in return? She serves them; she sets the meal before them. This type of mutual, willing service is what should characterize our hospitality. Husbands should serve their wives and wives their husbands; parents should serve their children and children their parents; hosts should serve their guests and guests their hosts. In this way, we will be able to fulfill Peter's admonition, "Be hospitable to one another *without grumbling*" (1 Pet. 4:8).[4]

Gifts to the Poor

Second, feast days are fitting days to bless others. Jesus' example in the Gospel of Mark teaches us that giving to others, especially to those in need, is a fitting adornment of the Sabbath.[5] Frequently we find Jesus healing on the Sabbath, as He does in

[4]It should be noted that there are many practical ways to reduce this burden and families should avail themselves of these means: having others bring portions of the meal, fixing the meal ahead of time, choosing simple recipes, using crock pots, joining all hands for cleaning, etc.

[5]These gifts have traditionally been labeled "works of mercy" in Reformed literature.

this text with Simon Peter's mother-in-law (vv. 30–31). Arriving at the home, He discovers that Simon's mother-in-law is ill with a fever. Luke the physician calls it a *pureto megalo*, a "very high fever" (cf. Lk. 4:38). She is so sick that she is unable to get out of bed. And so Jesus comes, takes her by the hand, and lifts her up—healing her to such an extent that it is as though the fever had never afflicted her, because she immediately sets about serving them their Sabbath meal.

Mark concludes his story of Jesus' Sabbath Day by recording other acts of mercy. In the evening, after the Sabbath was over (so that the Pharisaic restrictions on bearing burdens would no longer apply), many people came to Simon's house bringing folks in need of healing—both of their various illnesses and of their demonic afflictions.

> [32]At evening, when the sun had set, they brought to Him all who were sick and those who were demon-possessed. [33]And the whole city was gathered together at the door. [34]Then He healed many who were sick with various diseases, and cast out many demons; and He did not allow the demons to speak, because they knew Him. (Mk. 1:32–34)

Jesus extends mercy and grace to these folks on the Sabbath, even as He will do later for the man with the withered hand (cf. Mk. 3:5–6). In opposition to the Pharisees who allowed only life-threatening illnesses to be treated on the Sabbath (cf. Lk. 13:10–17), Jesus healed any who were in need. As we have emphasized again and again, the Sabbath is a time for feasting, rejoicing, and thanking God—so what more appropriate day to give to those in need? Paul applied this to Christian worship by encouraging the Corinthians to take a special offering on the Lord's Day for the Jerusalem church (cf. 1 Cor. 16:1–2). The Lord's Day is about deliverance. It is Gospel, good news. God has acted in Christ to rescue us, to heal us, to restore us.

Consequently, it is most fitting to extend mercy to others on this day when we celebrate the many mercies that have been and continue to be extended to us by our Creator and Redeemer.

This is basic Gospel logic. We love because God first loved us; having been forgiven, we forgive; having been blessed, we bless. This is why the feasts throughout the Old Testament included the giving of gifts to those in need. Ezra and Nehemiah encouraged the people at the Feast of Trumpets to "send portions to those for whom nothing is prepared" (Neh. 8:10). Likewise, Mordecai and the Jews established the Feast of Purim "as the days on which [they] had rest from their enemies, as the month which was turned from sorrow to joy for them, and from mourning to a holiday; that they should make them days of feasting and joy, of *sending presents to one another and gifts to the poor*" (Est. 9:22). What better way to display the grace that has been given to us than by extending it to others?

Jesus, therefore, shows us the beauty of active mercy. He casts out demons; He heals Peter's mother-in-law and many others; He restores the man with the withered hand—all of this on the Sabbath. According to Peter, Jesus "went about doing good and healing all who were oppressed by the devil, for God was with Him" (Acts 10:38). Jesus actively practiced mercy. Doing good is lawful on the Sabbath, and so He looked for good to do.

And let us not forget that one way we extend this grace and mercy to others is by allowing them to rest: "Six days you shall do your work, and on the seventh day you shall rest, that your ox and your donkey may rest, and the son of your female servant and the stranger *may be refreshed*" (Exod. 23:12). Business owners, executives, and politicians, in particular, should grant mercy to those dependent upon them by granting the Lord's Day as a day of refreshment. Indeed, the grace of Sabbath rest prevents many of the stress-related illnesses that plague society and that necessitate other works of mercy.[6]

Note, therefore, that there is a healthy silence in Mark's account of Jesus' Sabbath life. What happened after Jesus exited the synagogue and before folks came to him in the evening for healing? Aside from fellowship and feasting with friends, Mark does not give us much information—and this is fitting. Why? Because the Sabbath was given as a time of rest and refreshment. In six days God created the heavens and the earth and all that is in them and on the seventh day *He rested.* He looked upon His labors and took delight in them, enjoying them (cf. Gen. 2:2–3). As Doug Wilson has written and remarked, the fourth commandment does not tell us to work six days in one way and then the seventh in another; it tells us to rest.[7]

Nevertheless, some have argued that the Sabbath is a day to do "spiritual" work, while the other six days are given for "secular" work. The Westminster Confession, for example, could be read this way. It notes that to honor the Sabbath truly, believers should be "taken up, *the whole time,* in the public and private exercises of [God's] worship, and in the duties of necessity and mercy."[8] Likewise, the Westminster Shorter Catechism insists that the Lord's Day is honored by *"spending the whole time* in the public and private exercises of God's worship."[9] If a narrow

[6]The plethora of religious and secular titles addressing the problems of stress and overload frequently overlook a basic answer to our problems: we are stressed and overloaded because we simply do not know how to rest, and this is precisely what the Lord's Day teaches us.

[7]Douglas Wilson, *Mother Kirk: Essays on Church Life* (Moscow: Canon Press, 2001), 112–113.

[8]*The Westminster Confession of Faith,* XXI.8, emphasis added. A copy of the Westminster Confession and Catechisms can be found in Philip Schaff's *The Creeds of Christendom, Volume 3: The Evangelical and Protestant Creeds* (Grand Rapids: Baker Book House, 2007).

[9]*The Westminster Shorter Catechism,* Question 60. Emphasis added.

definition of God's worship—excluding physical rest, refreshment, and fellowship with God's people—is coupled with the phrase "the whole time," then we run the risk of laboring for seven days without resting. Mark's healthy silence about the actions of our Lord provides a corrective to this tendency and reminds us that the Sabbath was given for rest. As John Frame remarks, "The Sabbath rest is physical, not merely a ceasing of one activity in order to perform another, as some Reformed writers have represented it."[10]

Bear No Burden

But we have yet to interact directly with the types of restrictions on Lord's Day behavior illustrated in our opening scene from *Little House*. Does God forbid smiling and recreation on the Sabbath?

As we have studied the intent of the Sabbath and explored the metaphor of feasting, it should be apparent that the Sabbath was never intended to restrict such things. Yet, because the Pharisees treated the Sabbath as a fast rather than a feast, they distorted Old Testament Sabbath law and used it to prohibit many things that God did not—things as simple as traveling more than a certain distance or carrying burdens about. Unfortunately, many Christians through the ages have followed suit.

In the Gospels, we find Jesus routinely scorning these restrictions. He feasts and fellowships with His disciples. He permits Peter's mother-in-law to serve. He heals those in need (cf. Lk. 13:10ff; 14:1ff). He allows His disciples to rub kernels of grain in their hands to feed themselves (cf. Mk. 2:23ff). He treats the Sabbath as a feast, not a fast. It is a day to celebrate

[10]John Frame, *The Doctrine of the Christian Life* (Phillipsburg: P&R, 2008), 541.

the work of God by worshiping and fellowshipping with His people and helping those in need.

Consider two stories from the Gospel of John which illustrate Jesus' scorn for the Pharisees' restrictions. First, the healing of the man born blind. After the man was healed, the Jews declared that Jesus could not be from God because He was violating the Sabbath (9:16). His offense? Making clay on the Sabbath and applying it to the eyes of the man born blind (9:14). According to the Pharisees, this was work and therefore prohibited. But here's the fascinating question: why did Jesus make the clay? After all, He could have healed the man simply by His power (cf. Mk. 10:46ff). He made the clay purposefully to poke at the absurdity of the Pharisaic restrictions. They were straining a gnat and swallowing a camel.

The healing of the man at the Pool of Bethesda gives us another instance of Jesus' scorn for the Pharisaic Sabbath. Upon healing the man, Jesus commanded him, "Rise, take up your bed and walk" (Jn. 5:8). According to the Pharisees, however, carrying his bed was a violation of the Sabbath.

> [9]And that day was the Sabbath. [10]The Jews therefore said to him who was cured, "It is the Sabbath; it is not lawful for you to carry your bed." [11]He answered them, "He who made me well said to me, 'Take up your bed and walk.'" (Jn. 5:9–11)

The conduct of the man on this occasion was cause for much concern among the Jews. They were convinced that this man was violating a clear biblical precedent, and they had a verse to prove it. Jeremiah had commanded:

> [21]Thus says the Lord: "Take heed to yourselves, and bear no burden on the Sabbath day, nor bring it in by the gates of Jerusalem; [22]nor carry a burden out of your houses on the Sabbath day, nor do any work, but hallow the Sabbath day, as I commanded your fathers." (Jer. 17:21–22)

The Jews felt that Jesus' conduct was an obvious sign of His disobedience to God's will. Why else would He command the man to carry His bed? Jeremiah said not to bear a burden on the Sabbath, but Jesus commanded this man to carry His bed. One of them had to be wrong; the Jews concluded it was Jesus. There was, of course, another option: their understanding of Jeremiah could have been all wet.

And this was Jesus' contention. He saw that their interpretation of Jeremiah was frivolous and perverse, missing Jeremiah's whole point. Indeed, once again Jesus seems to be ruffling the Jews' feathers intentionally to force them to reconsider their position. Jeremiah did not forbid carrying things around on the Sabbath; such a notion is absurd. Rather, Jeremiah was condemning the perpetuation of business as usual on the Sabbath. Merchants were selling their wares, bringing them into Jerusalem, and making their profits. Likewise, Israelites themselves were bringing their wares out of their homes into the marketplace. The issue was not carrying items from one place to another but *continuing one's labors from the week.* "Six days you shall labor and do all your work." Commercial labor was to cease; life was not (cf. Neh. 13:15–22).

Our Lord repeatedly emphasized this point in His controversies with the Pharisees. They were trivializing the Sabbath by manufacturing burdens for the people of Israel that not even they themselves could bear. The Sabbath was given to protect the poor and needy. It was given to refresh the souls of men and teach them to rest, keeping them from madness. It was not intended to prohibit rubbing heads of grain in one's hands, nor to prevent the healing of those in need, nor to specify the types of objects that could be carried about the neighborhood.[11]

---

[11]The material in this section corresponds loosely to what Reformed writers have called "works of necessity." I have avoided this terminology because it can lead to reductionism. After all, what exactly is necessary (at least as we define that word today)? We might say it is "necessary" to drive

It was the regulation of these types of things that moved our Lord to oppose the Pharisees so strenuously. Jesus was no Sabbath breaker—yet the Pharisees, by their additions to the law, were convinced that He was. Jesus corrects them. The purpose of the Sabbath was first and foremost rest, refreshment, and restoration—healing for the body and the soul. Consequently, laborious work, exploitation of the poor and needy, and neglecting the worship of God would all violate the Sabbath. Feasting, smiling, playing, and celebrating would not.[12]

Finding Your Own Pleasure

But many may have nagging doubts about the portrayal of the Lord's Day that I have been giving thus far. It sounds too good to be true. The Sabbath a feast? The Lord's Day a time of celebration? Its absence a curse? How can these things be? Aren't we to avoid pursuing our own pleasures on this day? After all, the Lord declared through Isaiah:

> [13]If you turn away your foot from the Sabbath,
> From doing your pleasure on My holy day,
> And call the Sabbath a delight,

---

to church but certainly it is not "necessary" to take a drive around the lake. Therefore the former is permitted as a "work of necessity" but the latter forbidden. But this misses the whole point. The point is that the Lord's Day is a feast, a holy feast to celebrate and praise the Lord and strengthen His people. So enjoy, celebrate, rejoice—drive around the lake. But don't force Freddy to work that day to finance your drive or to cover your lack of forethought to get gas. For an excellent discussion of "works of necessity" consult John Frame, *The Doctrine of the Christian Life*, (Phillipsburg: P&R, 2008), 547–550.

[12]It is important to distinguish between recreation and organized sports. The former are a joy to the Lord (cf. Zech. 8:4–5). Part of feasting is sporting about, enjoying the day, throwing the Frisbee, sledding down the hill, shooting hoops, throwing horse shoes, playing tennis. It seems to me, however, that organized or league sports are decidedly different. In the former

> The holy day of the Lord honorable,
> And shall honor Him, not doing your own ways,
> Nor finding your own pleasure,
> Nor speaking your own words,
> [14]Then you shall delight yourself in the Lord;
> And I will cause you to ride on the high hills of the earth,
> And feed you with the heritage of Jacob your father.
> The mouth of the Lord has spoken. (Is. 58:13–14)

Some folks have used this passage to impose strict limitations upon any type of "pleasurable" activity on the Sabbath. No doubt it was this passage that inspired the supposed prohibition against laughing or even smiling on Sundays in the time of Laura's grandfather. What does Isaiah mean here by "not finding your own pleasure"? Does this undermine the case that the Sabbath is a feast and not a fast?

Not at all. We have already seen that Isaiah is very concerned about the Sabbath law because it was given by God to uphold justice.[13] The Sabbath preserved the weakest members of society from exploitation. Amos alludes to this in one of his oracles against the people of Israel:

> [4]Hear this, you who swallow up the needy,
> And make the poor of the land fail,
> [5]Saying:
> "When will the New Moon be past,
> That we may sell grain?
> And the Sabbath,

---

case, the recreation serves as a means of enjoying fellowship and feasting with the people of God. The focus can still be the Lord and His day. In the latter case, however, the sport has become the focus itself. No longer is it the means to the end, it is the end itself. While we may still get to church, the sense of reserving this day for the Lord and His people is gone. For my family, therefore, sports that include scheduled Sunday practices or games are out.

[13]See Chapter 1.

That we may trade wheat?
Making the ephah small and the shekel large,
Falsifying the scales by deceit,
⁶That we may buy the poor for silver,
And the needy for a pair of sandals—
Even sell the bad wheat?" (Amos 8:4–6)

The leaders in Israel were chafing at the Sabbath because it was preventing them from exploiting the poor. A close examination of Isaiah 58 reveals that it is this same problem he is addressing. His restriction on the "pleasures" of the people is not forbidding mirth and joy: it is forbidding exploitation and avarice. This is evident as we study Isaiah's rebuke of the Israelites' fasting earlier in the chapter. Rather than fast to show true contrition for their sin, the Israelites were putting on an external show. Isaiah rebukes them with these words, "In fact, in the day of your fast you find pleasure, and *exploit all your laborers*" (58:3b). In Hebraic parallelism, Isaiah indicates that the exploitation of the laborers *was* the pleasure that the people were finding. It is this same "pleasure" that the Israelites were to shun on the Sabbath. Oppressing the needy was forbidden; joy, refreshment, and recreation were not.[14]

After all, notice the imperative in Isaiah's text. The Israelites were to *call the Sabbath a delight*. They were to honor the Lord by honoring—setting apart—this day. What for? Not for their sinful pleasures, but for the worship of God, for the relief of the poor, for the imitation of their Redeemer. And they were not to do this crankily but with joy. For if they would call the Sabbath a delight, God would cause them to "delight" in Him (v. 14). Pleasure is not the problem; sin is.

---

[14]See John N. Oswalt, *The Book of Isaiah: Chapters 40–66,* New International Commentary on the Old Testament (Grand Rapids: Eerdmans, 1998), 508–509.

If we observe the Sabbath, then folks are going to ask questions. It's going to cause raised eyebrows. And there is nothing wrong with this. "Do you want to go golfing Sunday morning?" "Well, no thanks—I'd rather enter into heaven with the people of God and worship the Lord." "Huh?" But if we're doing it right, *if we're keeping the heart of the Sabbath while keeping the Sabbath,* then the nature of the questions should be those of longing; our practice should entice others and invite imitation. Our practice should be as tantalizing as our Lord Himself. Frequently, however, we, like the Pharisees, make the Sabbath look about as attractive as a hairless cat. "Ooh, yeah! I'd really like one of those." This should not be. Instead, our heart toward those who don't celebrate the Sabbath should be one of pity. "You poor thing, come rest a while, come see the glory of worshiping the Lord, come imitate the Creator. Let me show you how good life really can be."

Liberation or Restriction

This orientation of joy and gratitude helps us face the Lord's Day aright. Rather than focus on what we cannot do on the Lord's Day—which was one of the distortions of the Pharisees—Jesus' conduct focuses on what we get to do. "Is it lawful on the Sabbath to *do* good or to do evil, to *save life* or to kill?" We get to rest, we get to worship, we get to fellowship, we get to show mercy, we get to study the Word, we get to refresh our souls. Glory to God.

Look around at our culture. Look how harried and distracted people are. Look how busy and hamster-like people are. Look at who benefits the most from violating the Lord's Day, from unceasing labor—business owners and tax collectors. And in observing all this, observe the glory of Sabbath, the glory of the Lord's Day. The Lord's Day teaches us to rest; teaches us where prosperity comes from; teaches us where sanctification comes from. All these things come from the hand of God. So let us rest and watch Him work on our behalf. Remember Isaiah's promise to those who call the Sabbath a delight:

> [14]Then you shall delight yourself in the LORD;
> And I will cause you to ride on the high hills of the earth,
> And feed you with the heritage of Jacob your father.
> The mouth of the LORD has spoken. (Is. 58:14)

Our fundamental attitude individually toward the Lord's Day must be one of feasting, delight, liberation, and joy. And this is where our focus as communities should be as well. What should the Lord's Day look like? Again, what did the life of our Lord look like on this day? Prioritization of worship, devotion to teaching and fellowship with the people of God, participation in feasting and assisting others—*the very things that the institution of the Sabbath was given to cultivate and protect from the beginning.* So these are the types of things that should characterize us. And so what should our Lord's Day look like? Rest, worship, instruction, feasting, fellowship, mercy. These are our priorities; these are the things that characterize a typical Sabbath day.

Once we get this right, we're in a position to answer other related questions—should I work on the Lord's Day? If so, under what circumstances? Should I engage in organized sports? Should I patronize businesses? These are all important questions that need answers. But if we jump to these types of questions without getting the heart of the Lord's Day first—feasting, delight, liberation, worship, joy—then we will become nothing more than modern day Pharisees. The Lord's Day should be the best day of the week. "Huh? Run myself ragged on the Lord's Day? No thanks—I'd rather drive my clunker, feast with my family, and study God's Word."

And so, in our families, let us consider how to make the Lord's Day the best day of the week. Let us break out the fine china; fix the best food; drag out the sweets; open a bottle of good wine; invite friends and family; read and study and enjoy the Word of God together; and pray corporately with joy. The Lord's Day should be the best day of the week. So we should consider how to make it so given the ages of our children and the opportunities the Lord has placed before us.[15] And when we face some decision about what to do on the Lord's Day, we need to ask ourselves, is this thing that we are considering accentuating the feast or pulling us away from it?

Rest for the Soul

Finally, consider what the Christian Sabbath, the Lord's Day, teaches us as the people of God. The Lord's Day has a greater significance than itself. It is not given simply that we might be refreshed, simply that we might have a regular time to worship, simply that we might imitate our Creator. As we saw in our survey of our Lord's life on the Sabbath Day, the Sabbath was given to remind Israel that it was the Lord who set them apart, the Lord who sanctified them (cf. Exod. 31:13). The Sabbath reminded them to rest in God; to cease striving and know that He is God.

Jesus repeats this same promise in connection with himself. "Come to Me, all who are weary and heavy-laden, and I will give you rest" (Mt. 11:28, NASB). In Jesus we find rest—rest from sin, rest from guilt, rest from running away from God. Jesus is our

[15]For food for thought in these areas, consult some of the stimulating articles and talks by Doug Jones including "The Sabbath Wedding," *Credenda/Agenda,* Vol. 12, Issue 2. Also consult Marva J. Dawn, *Keeping the Sabbath Wholly: Ceasing, Resting, Embracing, Feasting* (Grand Rapids: Eerdmans, 1989).

Sabbath. The Lord's Day is our weekly reminder, "Hey, this isn't your own work. Jesus is the Good Shepherd and He knows His sheep and His sheep hear His voice and follow Him. And guess what? He will lose nothing of all the Father has given Him. So rejoice! Rejoice! Rejoice in the Savior. Remember His triumph over the grave on your behalf."

The Sabbath is a call to faith, a call to believe the One who has created us and who has rescued and redeemed us from slavery.

> Therefore, since a promise remains of entering His rest, let us fear lest any of you seem to have come short of it. For indeed the gospel was preached to us as well as to them; but the word which they heard did not profit them, not being mixed with faith in those who heard it. For we who have believed do enter that rest. (Heb. 4:1–3a)

Through faith we enter the everlasting rest, that rest which the Lord's Day only anticipates. But given the glory of that eternal rest, how glorious ought our rest on the Lord's Day be? Should our children complain like Laura that Sunday is here again? Should we not foster in ourselves and in our children a longing for the Lord's Day, a longing for this day that is the best day of the week? For our diligence to enter the weekly rest on the Lord's Day mirrors our determination to enter our final rest. "Let us therefore be diligent to enter that rest" (Heb. 4:11a).

More from Canon Press

Because hospitality both teaches and gives pleasure, it will provide many holy memories to children. Children should remember more about their youth than just holidays, vacations, and the things they received for Christmas or birthdays. They should grow with traditions and memories that actually mold their perspective and stand out to guide their future lives. . . .

Thousands of little experiences like this, when taken together, have an enormous effect on our children's thinking. They will grow up with a complex and intuitive knowledge of generosity and friendship. They should have cheery memories of sharing food and conversation with hundreds of saints throughout the years. They should know the Lord's day as the great weekly day of celebration. Experiences like this change lives, and indeed will change the entire culture, when they are remembered and recalled as a model for the future. When your children think back on their childhood, they should want their household to be as godly. This familial obedience and celebration will change the world, not lectures or conferences or even sermons. These things will change the world, but they cannot be taught. They must be shown, exemplified, and demonstrated.

FACE TO FACE
Meditations on Friendship and Hospitality
by Steve Wilkins

CPSIA information can be obtained at www.ICGtesting.com
Printed in the USA
BVOW04s2105191213

339472BV00008B/437/P